BY MIKKI WYATT

THE ALL-OUT GUIDE
MAXIMIZE
Your Short–Term
Rental Profits

MIKKI WYATT

Maximize Your Short-Term Rental Profits

The All-Out Guide

This book was professionally typeset on Reedsy.
Find out more at reedsy.com

one word: Begin.

Much love to my husband, Thomas, and my family.

Contents

Preface

Welcome to the world of short-term rentals, where the opportunities for profitability abound. Whether you're a seasoned property owner or a newcomer looking to dive into the lucrative world of short-term rentals, this book is your comprehensive guide to unlocking the secrets of success. From choosing the right property to marketing strategies and guest satisfaction, we've got you covered.

How to Use This Book:

This is a guide to the wide and varied world of Short-term rentals, also known as "Airbnb" rentals. This book will help you make important decisions and explain all the complicated aspects that go along with this field. This book is a bible: it's a go-to all-in-one-place resource.

This book is broken down into eight sections, with overlaps in many areas, so you can choose a section and start there if it's an area you need to focus on and then move on to another area.

Take the time to read each one to outline where you need to go. Make notes in the margins.

Have a great adventure!

1

Chapter 1: Understanding the Short-Term Rental Market

1. Overview of the Short-Term Rental Market

Market Growth

The short-term rental market has experienced significant growth in recent years, driven by the rise of online platforms such as Airbnb, Vrbo, and Booking.com. This growth can be attributed to changing travel preferences, a desire for unique accommodations, and the convenience offered by online booking platforms.

Diversification of Offerings

Short-term rentals are no longer limited to traditional vacation destinations. Urban areas, suburbs, and even rural locations have seen an increase in short-term rental offerings. This diversification caters to many travelers, including business professionals, families, and individuals seeking unique experiences.

Impact of COVID

The global pandemic profoundly impacted the travel and hospitality industry, including short-term rentals. Initially, there was a downturn in bookings due to travel restrictions and safety concerns. However, as restrictions eased, there was a trend toward domestic travel, and short-term rentals became popular choices for those seeking private and socially distanced accommodations.

Regulatory Challenges

Regulatory challenges have been recurring in the short-term rental market. Many cities and regions have implemented or considered regulations to address housing availability, neighborhood disturbances, and safety standards. Hosts need to be aware of and comply with local regulations.

Professionalization of Hosts

The market has seen a shift toward more professional hosting, with some hosts managing multiple properties and even forming small property management companies. This professionalization reflects the quality of accommodations and services offered.

Technology and Data Analytics

Hosts increasingly utilize technology and data analytics to optimize pricing, enhance the guest experience, and efficiently manage operations. Dynamic pricing tools, smart home devices, and analytics platforms contribute to the overall growth and competitiveness of the market.

Customer Expectations

As the market matures, customer expectations for short-term rentals have risen. Guests now seek high-quality amenities, cleanliness, and personalized experiences. Hosts who prioritize guest satisfaction will see increased bookings and positive reviews.

In conclusion, the short-term rental market continues evolving, presenting opportunities and challenges for hosts. Staying informed about market trends, understanding local regulations, and adapting to changing consumer preferences are crucial for success in this dynamic industry. Consider consulting recent market reports and industry updates for the latest and most accurate information.

2. Key factors influencing demand

The demand for short-term rentals is influenced by various factors that cater to the preferences and needs of travelers. Key factors significantly shape the demand for short-term rentals

Location

Selecting an optimal location for a short-term rental is a crucial factor that significantly influences the success of the venture. A good location aligns with the preferences of the target guest demographic, offers convenience, and provides unique attractions or experiences. Proximity to popular tourist destinations, local amenities, and public transportation can enhance the property's appeal. Understanding the local market demand and considering the safety and security of the neighborhood are also vital aspects. Additionally, taking into account any regulatory requirements for short-term rentals in the chosen location is essential for compliance. A strategic location not only attracts guests but also contributes to positive reviews, repeat bookings, and overall profitability, making it a cornerstone in the overall success of a short-term rental business.

Property Type and Amenities

Choosing the right type of property and amenities for a short-term rental is pivotal in creating a desirable and competitive offering. The property type should align with the target audience's preferences, whether it's a cozy apartment for solo travelers, a family-friendly home, or a luxury villa for upscale guests. Considering the local market demand and the purpose of visitation to the area is crucial for making informed decisions. Equally important are the amenities provided, which can greatly impact guest satisfaction. Offering essentials like comfortable bedding, well-equipped kitchens, and Wi-Fi is standard, but additional amenities such as a swimming pool, parking, or pet-friendly facilities can set a property apart. Striking the right balance between essential comforts and unique, value-added amenities ensures that the short-term rental not only meets but exceeds guest expectations, leading to positive reviews and

4

increased demand.

Pricing

Pricing is critical to managing a successful short-term rental, and adopting a competitive and reasonable pricing strategy is key to attracting guests. It's essential to position the rental in a way that offers value compared to hotels and other accommodations in the area. Additionally, implementing dynamic pricing strategies allows for flexibility in adjusting rates based on demand fluctuations and seasonality. During peak times or high-demand periods, rates should be adjusted upward to maximize profitability, while off-peak or low-demand periods may see more competitive pricing to maintain occupancy. This dynamic approach ensures that the property remains appealing to a diverse range of guests while optimizing revenue potential. Striking the right balance between competitive pricing and value-added offerings contributes to the overall success of the short-term rental by attracting guests and fostering positive reviews.

Online Presence and Marketing

Establishing a strong online presence and implementing effective marketing strategies are crucial elements in maximizing the success of a short-term rental. The quality of online listings plays a pivotal role, emphasizing the importance of attractive photos and detailed, engaging descriptions that showcase the property's unique features. Positive reviews and high ratings from previous guests build credibility and influence potential guests' decision-making. Leveraging popular platforms such as Airbnb, Vrbo, Booking.com, and others is essential for reaching a broader audience. Implementing effective marketing strategies on these platforms, including optimizing listings for search algorithms, using competitive pricing, and promoting special offers, can significantly enhance visibility. A well-managed online presence attracts bookings and contributes to a positive reputation, encouraging repeat business and referrals. A dynamic interplay of quality content, guest feedback, and strategic marketing positions a short-term rental for sustained success in the competitive hospitality market.

Travel Trends and Seasons

Remaining attuned to current travel trends and seasonal demand variations are integral to the success of a short-term rental business. Adapting to contemporary travel trends, including the growing popularity of remote work and digital nomadism, allows property owners to tailor their offerings to meet the evolving needs of the modern traveler. Short-term rentals can capitalize on the increasing number of individuals seeking alternative accommodation solutions by providing amenities conducive to remote work and flexible booking options. Additionally, understanding seasonal demand variations and events that attract travelers is vital for optimizing pricing strategies and occupancy rates. Whether catering to summer vacationers, winter holidaymakers, or attendees of local events, aligning the short-term rental with the ebbs and flows of travel patterns ensures a consistent and profitable business model that resonates with diverse guest demographics.

Flexibility and Convenience

Providing flexibility and convenience is a cornerstone of creating a positive guest experience in the short-term rental industry. Offering flexible check-in and check-out options caters to the diverse schedules of guests, accommodating early arrivals or late departures. This flexibility enhances guests' overall satisfaction, contributing to positive reviews and repeat bookings. Additionally, ensuring convenient access to public transportation, airports, or major highways is essential for attracting guests who prioritize ease of travel. Proximity to transportation hubs enhances the property's appeal and aligns with the evolving needs of travelers seeking seamless and efficient journeys. Short-term rentals can establish themselves as attractive and hassle-free accommodation choices for a wide range of guests by prioritizing flexibility in arrival and departure logistics and ensuring convenient access to transportation.

Health and Safety Considerations

Health and safety considerations have become paramount in the short-term rental industry, emphasizing the importance of cleanliness and property hygiene. Maintaining a high standard of cleanliness enhances the overall guest experience and contributes to the health and well-being of occupants. In the post-COVID-19 era, there is a heightened awareness of the need for rigorous health and safety measures. Property owners and managers are implementing enhanced cleaning protocols, sanitation practices, and contactless check-in procedures to ensure the safety of guests. Communicating these measures transparently in property listings builds trust and reassures guests of their well-being during their stay. By prioritizing health and safety considerations, short-term rentals meet evolving guest expectations and contribute to a responsible and resilient approach in the face of global health challenges.

Regulatory Compliance

Adherence to local regulations and licensing requirements is fundamental to operating a successful short-term rental. Property owners must stay informed about and comply with the specific rules and legal obligations governing short-term rentals in their respective locations.

This includes obtaining any necessary permits or licenses required by local authorities. Transparency in communication with guests regarding rules and expectations is equally crucial. Providing clear guidelines on house rules, occupancy limits, and specific requirements helps manage guest expectations and fosters a positive and compliant environment. By prioritizing regulatory compliance and transparent communication, short-term rentals avoid potential legal issues and build trust with guests, leading to positive reviews and repeat business.

Guest Experience

Ensuring a memorable guest experience is paramount for the success of a short-term rental. Positive past guest experiences and glowing reviews contribute significantly to the property's reputation and attractiveness to potential guests. Maintaining prompt and effective communication with guests from the booking stage through check-out is crucial in addressing inquiries, concerns, or special requests. Personalization and attention to detail in guest services, such as providing welcome amenities or local recommendations tailored to the guest's preferences, elevate the overall stay. Short-term rentals garner positive feedback and cultivate a loyal customer base by prioritizing guest satisfaction. The combination of positive reviews, excellent communication, and personalized services fosters a positive image that sets the property apart and encourages guests to choose it for their future stays.

Technology Integration

Technology integration is pivotal in enhancing the efficiency and guest experience in the short-term rental industry. Property owners leverage technology for seamless bookings through online platforms, simplifying the reservation process for guests. Additionally, the adoption of smart home features and devices adds a layer of convenience and sophistication to the guest experience. Automated check-in processes, keyless entry systems, and smart home controls contribute to a frictionless stay. Moreover, technology facilitates effective communication between hosts and guests, allowing quick responses to inquiries and efficient resolution of issues. By embracing these technological advancements, short-term rentals not only streamline operational processes but also cater to the preferences of tech-savvy guests, thereby staying competitive in the dynamic hospitality landscape.

Cultural and Local Experiences

Providing cultural and local experiences is a key differentiator for short-term rentals, adding value to guests seeking an authentic immersion into the destination. Short-term rental hosts have the opportunity to offer unique and personalized experiences that reflect the richness of the local culture. This can include curated local activities, recommendations for authentic cuisine, or even organizing cultural events. The proximity of the rental property to cultural attractions, restaurants, and entertainment options further enhances the guest experience, allowing them to explore and engage with the local community easily. By integrating cultural elements into the guest stay and ensuring convenient access to local experiences, short-term rentals create a distinctive and memorable environment that sets them apart in the competitive hospitality market.

Family-Friendly Features

Incorporating family-friendly features is essential for short-term rentals that appeal to various guests, including families with children. Providing amenities specifically designed for families, such as child-friendly spaces, cribs, and games, enhances the overall experience for parents and children alike. Safety and security considerations are essential, with hosts implementing measures to ensure a secure environment, including childproofing, secure locks, and clear safety guidelines. By prioritizing the unique needs of families, short-term rentals not only attract a broader audience and foster positive guest experiences. Attention to family-friendly features demonstrates a commitment to accommodating the needs of diverse travelers, contributing to positive reviews and increased guest satisfaction.

Understanding and adapting to these factors can help short-term rental hosts attract diverse guests and maximize their property's occupancy and profitability.

3. Identifying profitable locations and property types

Identifying profitable locations and property types is crucial for success in the short-term rental market. Here are key considerations when determining where to invest and what property type to offer:

Research Local Demand

Conducting thorough research on local demand is a strategic step in optimizing the success of short-term rentals. Property owners must analyze local and regional tourism trends, understanding the dynamics of visitor preferences and the peak seasons for travel. Identifying popular destinations and areas with high demand for short-term rentals allows hosts to align their properties with the preferences of potential guests. This research empowers property owners to make informed decisions regarding property location, pricing strategies, and amenities, ultimately maximizing occupancy rates and profitability. By staying attuned to the ever-changing landscape of local demand, short-term rentals can position themselves as attractive options for travelers seeking accommodation in sought-after destinations.

Proximity to Attractions

Selecting a location with proximity to attractions is a crucial aspect of positioning a short-term rental for success. Optimal choices include areas near popular tourist attractions, bustling business districts, event venues, or iconic landmarks. The convenience of being close to these points of interest not only enhances the overall guest experience but also attracts a diverse range of travelers. Additionally, considering accessibility to public transportation and major highways further amplifies the appeal, making it easier for guests to explore the surrounding area. By strategically choosing a location with proximity to attractions and ensuring ease of travel, short-term rentals can capitalize on the desirability of their locale, contributing to increased bookings and positive guest feedback.

Check Regulatory Environment

Thoroughly checking the regulatory environment is a critical step in the success of short-term rentals. Property owners must conduct comprehensive research on local regulations and zoning laws for short-term rentals in their area. Understanding and adhering to these regulations is essential to avoid legal issues and ensure smooth operations. Additionally, hosts should ensure compliance with licensing requirements, obtaining any necessary permits or licenses as mandated by local authorities. By staying informed about and following the regulatory framework, short-term rentals mitigate the risk of legal challenges and foster a responsible and sustainable approach to their business operations within the community.

Understand Seasonal Demand

Understanding seasonal demand is crucial for short-term rentals to optimize yearly offerings. Property owners should consider the destination's seasonality, assessing whether it attracts tourists consistently or experiences specific peak seasons. This knowledge enables hosts to adapt their pricing and marketing strategies accordingly. During high-demand seasons, prices can be adjusted to maximize profitability, while off-peak periods may benefit from competitive pricing to maintain occupancy. By aligning strategies with seasonal variations, short-term rentals can cater to the changing needs of travelers and ensure a consistent flow of bookings throughout the year. This adaptability to seasonal demand contributes to the overall success and sustainability of the short-term rental business.

Analyze Competitor Landscape

Conducting a thorough analysis of the competitor landscape is crucial in positioning a short-term rental for success. Property owners should assess the competition within their chosen location, identifying other nearby rentals or accommodations. This analysis helps in understanding market trends, pricing strategies, and the unique features offered by competitors. By identifying gaps in the market or recognizing unique selling points, hosts can strategically position their property to stand out. Whether offering distinctive amenities, providing exceptional services, or targeting a specific niche, understanding the competitive landscape allows short-term rentals to differentiate themselves, attract a broader audience, and create a compelling value proposition for potential guests.

Property Type

Selecting the right property type is a fundamental decision that shapes the success of a short-term rental. It's essential to align the property type with the preferences and needs of the target audience. Whether catering to families, business travelers, vacationers, or a niche market, understanding the demographic allows hosts to tailor the property accordingly. Property owners should explore various options, considering apartments, houses, villas, or even unique accommodations like cabins or houseboats. Each property type offers distinct advantages, and the choice should reflect the local market demand and the specific desires of potential guests. By carefully considering the property type, short-term rentals can create an appealing and tailored experience, maximizing their attractiveness to the target audience and optimizing occupancy rates.

Amenities and Features

Choosing the right amenities and features is pivotal in enhancing the appeal and competitiveness of a short-term rental. Hosts should strategically offer amenities that cater to the preferences of their target guests, ensuring a comfortable and enjoyable stay. Common amenities like fully equipped kitchens, Wi-Fi, parking, and outdoor spaces are often expected and contribute to positive guest experiences. Additionally, considering unique features that set the property apart can be a key differentiator. This could include specialized amenities like a hot tub, smart home features, or access to exclusive local experiences. By carefully curating a combination of essential and distinctive amenities, short-term rentals not only meet the basic needs of guests but also create a memorable and standout experience, fostering positive reviews and guest satisfaction.

Budget-Friendly Options

Recognizing the demand for budget-friendly options is crucial for short-term rentals that cater to a diverse audience. Property owners should assess the local market to understand the needs of cost-conscious travelers and adapt their offerings accordingly. Consideration should be given to providing smaller units or shared spaces, which can be attractive to budget-conscious individuals or groups. Offering affordable alternatives without compromising on essential amenities ensures that the short-term rental remains competitive. By tapping into the demand for budget-friendly options, hosts can broaden their customer base, appeal to a wider range of travelers, and establish themselves as versatile and inclusive accommodation choice in the hospitality landscape.

Business Districts for Corporate Travelers

Exploring locations near business districts is a strategic approach for short-term rentals targeting corporate travelers. Proximity to business hubs enhances the property's appeal for professionals seeking convenient accommodation during work-related visits. Hosts can strategically highlight features that cater to the needs of corporate travelers, such as a dedicated workspace, high-speed internet, and proximity to conference centers or key business events. By positioning the short-term rental as a business-friendly option, hosts can tap into corporate travelers' demand to seek comfortable and well-equipped spaces that align with their professional requirements. This strategic focus attracts a specific niche market and positions the property as a preferred choice for business-related stays.

Analyze Airbnb Data

Leveraging Airbnb data analytics, such as Airbnb Insights or other relevant platforms, is a valuable strategy for short-term rental hosts to gain insights into demand, occupancy rates, and pricing dynamics in specific neighborhoods. By analyzing this data, hosts can make informed decisions about their property, including setting competitive pricing based on local market trends and optimizing occupancy rates. Identifying peak demand periods allows hosts to adjust pricing during high-traffic times, maximizing revenue potential strategically. Additionally, understanding the preferences of guests in specific neighborhoods can inform property management decisions, ensuring that the short-term rental aligns with the expectations of its target audience. This data-driven approach empowers hosts to adapt to the ever-changing dynamics of the short-term rental market and make strategic decisions that contribute to the overall success of their business.

Consider Evolving Trends

Staying attuned to evolving travel trends is essential for short-term rental hosts seeking long-term success. By keeping abreast of emerging destinations and travel preferences, hosts can proactively adapt their property type and location to meet the changing needs of travelers. This adaptability might involve diversifying property offerings to align with the latest trends, whether catering to remote work needs, eco-friendly accommodations, or unique experiential stays. Adapting to evolving traveler preferences allows hosts to position their properties as current and desirable options in the dynamic hospitality landscape. This forward-thinking approach ensures continued relevance and positions short-term rentals to capitalize on emerging opportunities in the ever-evolving travel industry.

Urban vs. Rural Considerations

When deciding on the location of short-term rentals, hosts should carefully assess whether their target audience prefers urban or rural settings. Understanding the preferences of potential guests is crucial in tailoring the property offerings to meet their expectations. Some travelers may seek the vibrancy and convenience of urban environments, while others may desire the tranquility and scenic beauty of rural settings. Hosts can consider offering properties in urban and rural locations to maximize the appeal to a diverse range of travelers. This approach broadens the potential customer base and allows hosts to tap into different market segments. By providing diverse options, short-term rentals can cater to the varied preferences of travelers, ensuring a more inclusive and successful business model.

Evaluate Local Infrastructure

Evaluating local infrastructure is a critical step for short-term rental hosts to ensure the smooth operation of their properties. It's imperative to verify that the local infrastructure provides reliable utilities and robust internet connectivity, as these are essential amenities for guests. A seamless and dependable infrastructure contributes to a positive guest experience and fosters satisfaction. Additionally, hosts should consider the availability of services such as cleaning and maintenance to uphold the property's standards. Reliable local services ensure that the short-term rental remains well-maintained and can address any issues promptly. By thoroughly assessing and ensuring the adequacy of local infrastructure, hosts can provide a consistent and reliable experience for guests, ultimately contributing to the success and sustainability of their short-term rental business.

By carefully considering these factors, you can identify locations and property types that align with market demand, ensuring the profitability of your short-term rental investment.

4. Researching local regulations and legal considerations

Researching and understanding local regulations and legal considerations is crucial for anyone involved in the short-term rental business. Here are steps to ensure compliance:

Check Zoning Laws

Before embarking on a short-term rental venture, it's imperative to thoroughly check local zoning laws to ensure compliance with regulations in the chosen operational area. Zoning laws can significantly impact the permissibility of using properties for short-term rentals, with different zones having varying regulations. Some areas may have specific restrictions or requirements related to the duration and nature of rentals. Investigating and understanding these regulations is crucial to avoid potential legal issues and ensure a smooth and lawful operation. Hosts can make informed decisions about property selection and operational strategies by conducting due diligence on local zoning laws, laying the foundation for a successful and legally compliant short-term rental business.

Licensing and Permits

Before embarking on a short-term rental venture, hosts should initiate inquiries about the essential licenses and permits necessary for operation. Recognizing that different cities or municipalities may impose specific requirements that hosts must meet to offer short-term accommodations legally is crucial. These requirements could encompass obtaining the appropriate business licenses, adhering to zoning regulations, ensuring compliance with safety standards, and securing permits for transient lodging. By proactively engaging in this due diligence and obtaining the requisite licenses and permits, hosts demonstrate a commitment to legal and regulatory compliance and contribute to the overall responsible and ethical growth of their short-term rental business within the community. This proactive approach helps ensure a smooth and lawful operation that aligns with the local regulations and fosters a positive relationship between hosts and the community.

Tax Obligations

Hosts venturing into short-term rentals should diligently familiarize themselves with the tax obligations linked to their specific location. It is imperative to comprehend the various taxes associated with short-term rentals, including occupancy taxes, sales taxes, or other local levies imposed on rental income. Local jurisdictions often have specific tax regulations applicable to short-term accommodations, and hosts are expected to fulfill these obligations to remain in compliance with the law. By understanding and adhering to the relevant tax requirements, hosts ensure legal compliance and contribute to the financial sustainability of their short-term rental venture. Seeking professional guidance and staying informed about tax regulation changes ensures hosts navigate the complex landscape of tax obligations responsibly and proactively.

Health and Safety Standards

Prioritizing health and safety standards is paramount for hosts operating short-term rentals. It is crucial to ensure compliance with various regulations, encompassing fire safety protocols, building codes, and occupancy limits dictated by local authorities. Hosts should proactively install necessary safety features, such as smoke detectors and fire extinguishers, to create a secure environment for guests. Providing comprehensive emergency information, including evacuation procedures and contact details, also contributes to a prepared and informed guest experience. By upholding rigorous health and safety standards, hosts not only comply with legal requirements but also demonstrate a commitment to the well-being of their guests. This proactive approach establishes trust, fosters positive guest experiences, and contributes to the overall success and reputation of the short-term rental within the community.

Noise Regulations

Navigating local noise regulations is essential for hosts operating short-term rentals to foster positive community relations. Being aware of and adhering to these regulations is crucial to prevent disturbances to neighbors. Hosts should establish clear guidelines for guests, emphasizing the importance of maintaining an appropriate noise level during their stay. Including specific quiet hours in the house rules provides a structured framework for managing noise and ensuring that guests consider their surroundings. By proactively addressing noise concerns and aligning with local regulations, hosts contribute to a harmonious living environment, mitigate potential conflicts with neighbors, and uphold the reputation of their short-term rental within the community. Clear communication and adherence to noise regulations help create a positive experience for guests while respecting the peace and tranquility of the neighborhood.

Insurance Requirements

Hosts entering the realm of short-term rentals should thoroughly review insurance requirements associated with their specific location. Different jurisdictions may impose specific insurance mandates, and hosts must understand and comply with these regulations. Ensuring that the short-term rental has adequate coverage protects the property and its contents, aligns with local regulations, and mitigates potential liabilities. Hosts should consider insurance options covering property damage, liability, and potential guest injuries. By proactively addressing insurance requirements, hosts safeguard their investment and con-tribute to the responsible and lawful operation of their short-term rental business within the community. Seeking professional advice and staying informed about any changes in insurance regulations ensures hosts navigate this aspect of their business responsibly and effectively.

Accessibility Compliance

Ensuring accessibility compliance is crucial for hosts operating short-term rentals, particularly to accommodate individuals with disabilities. Hosts should verify whether their property aligns with accessibility stan-dards, which may include providing accessible entrances, bathrooms, and other facilities as per local regulations and the Americans with Disabilities Act (ADA) in the United States. Taking steps to enhance acces-sibility meets legal requirements and broadens the property's appeal to a diverse range of guests. Clear communication of accessibility features in property listings fosters transparency and helps guests make informed decisions based on their needs. By prioritizing accessibility compliance, hosts contribute to creating an inclusive and welcoming environment, enhancing the overall experience for guests while adhering to ethical and legal considerations in short-term rental operations.

Landlord-Tenant Laws

Hosts engaged in short-term rentals must thoroughly familiarize themselves with landlord-tenant laws specific to their area. Understanding hosts' and guests' rights and responsibilities is crucial for maintaining a lawful and transparent operation. This includes being well-versed in eviction procedures, security deposit regulations, and other legal aspects. Adhering to these laws not only ensures hosts operate within the bounds of the legal framework but also contributes to establishing clear expectations for both parties involved. Proactive knowledge of landlord-tenant laws helps hosts navigate potential challenges, such as dispute resolution and fosters a fair and responsible short-term rental environment. Staying informed about changes in local regulations ensures hosts remain compliant with evolving legal requirements, ultimately contributing to their short-term rental business's sustained success and positive reputation.

Community Association Rules

For hosts operating short-term rentals, especially those within home-owners associations (HOA) or community associations, it is imperative to thoroughly review and adhere to the established rules and restrictions governing such rentals. Many associations have specific guidelines to regulate short-term rental activities within the community. Hosts should familiarize themselves with these rules, which may cover aspects like guest parking, noise regulations, and property aesthetics. Complying with community association rules ensures legal and contractual obligations are met and fosters positive relations with neighbors and the broader community. Proactive engagement with the association and clear communication of short-term rental activities help maintain a harmonious living environment and contribute to the community's overall well-being.

Code of Conduct and Ethics

Maintaining a strong code of conduct and adhering to ethical business practices are foundational principles for hosts engaged in short-term rentals. Establishing and upholding high standards of behavior contributes to the business's professionalism and fosters trust among guests, neighbors, and the local community. Building positive relationships with neighbors is crucial to minimize potential conflicts and ensure a harmonious living environment. Hosts should prioritize open communication, respond promptly to concerns, and take proactive measures to address any issues that may arise. By prioritizing ethical conduct and positive engagement, hosts contribute to the community's overall well-being, create a positive reputation for their short-term rental business, and establish a foundation for sustained success in the competitive hospitality landscape.

Environmental Regulations

Hosts involved in short-term rentals should be conscientious of environmental regulations applicable to their property. It is crucial to stay informed about any environmental guidelines that may govern waste disposal, energy usage, or other eco-friendly practices. Ensuring compliance with these regulations aligns with legal requirements and demonstrates a commitment to sustainable and responsible business practices. Hosts should implement proper waste disposal methods, encourage energy-efficient measures, and consider eco-friendly initiatives that contribute to preserving the local environment. By incorporating environmentally conscious practices into short-term rental operations, hosts meet regulatory standards and appeal to a growing market of eco-conscious travelers, fostering a positive image for their property and contributing to the broader goal of sustainable hospitality.

Stay Informed About Changes

Remaining informed about changes or updates to local regulations is essential for hosts engaged in short-term rentals. The regulatory landscape for short-term rentals can evolve, and hosts must stay abreast of any modifications to ensure continued legal compliance. Joining local host associations or forums provides a valuable platform for hosts to stay connected with updates in the short-term rental community. Engaging with these networks allows hosts to share insights, exchange information, and receive timely updates on any changes in regulations, industry trends, or best practices. This proactive approach ensures hosts are well-prepared to adapt their operations to evolving circumstances, fostering a resilient and informed short-term rental business.

In the dynamic landscape of short-term rentals, it is crucial to recognize the significant variations in regulations across different locations. Hosts planning to operate in this space should conduct thorough research specific to the area of operation, considering the diverse legal requirements that may exist. Seeking guidance from local authorities, legal professionals, or industry associations becomes imperative in gaining valuable insights and navigating the intricacies of specific regulations. Hosts can ensure legal compliance, foster positive community relations, and establish a solid foundation for a successful and responsible short-term rental business by adopting a proactive approach and staying well-informed about the local regulatory environment.

2

Chapter 2: Property Selection and Preparation

5. Choosing the right property for short-term rentals

Choosing the right property for short-term rentals is a crucial step that can significantly impact your success as a host. Here are essential considerations to help you make an informed decision. Firstly, assess the property's location – opt for areas with high demand and proximity to popular attractions or business districts. Understand the target market you aim to attract, whether families, business travelers, or vacationers, and tailor the property to their needs. Additionally, evaluate the property's size and layout, ensuring it aligns with your target audience's preferences. Consider local regulations regarding short-term rentals, ensuring compliance to avoid legal complications. Finally, consider the property's overall condition and potential for improvement – a well-maintained and aesthetically pleasing space can significantly enhance its appeal to guests.

Research Market Demand

Researching market demand is pivotal in establishing a successful short-term rental business. Begin by identifying areas with high demand for such accommodations, focusing on popular tourist destinations, bustling business districts, or regions with unique attractions. Conduct a thorough analysis of market trends, taking into account the preferences and behaviors of your target audience. By staying attuned to the ebb and flow of demand in specific locations and understanding the evolving needs of potential guests, you can strategically position your short-term rental to meet market expectations and maximize occupancy rates.

Location, Location, Location

The adage "Location, Location, Location" holds immense significance in the realm of short-term rentals. Optimal success lies in choosing a location that aligns with the convenience and preferences of your target guests. Proximity to public transportation, popular tourist attractions, vibrant restaurants, and bustling shopping centers can significantly enhance the property's overall appeal. By strategically situating your short-term rental in a location that caters to the needs and desires of your intended audience, you not only increase the likelihood of attracting guests but also elevate their overall experience, setting the stage for positive reviews and sustained business growth.

Understand Zoning Laws

A thorough understanding of zoning laws is imperative to short-term rental success. Before establishing your property in a chosen area, conducting comprehensive research on local zoning laws is crucial to ensure that short-term rentals are permitted. Different zones may have specific regulations regarding property use, and staying informed about these legal considerations is paramount. By familiarizing yourself with local zoning laws, you not only safeguard your business from potential legal complications but also demonstrate a commitment to compliance and responsible hosting practices. This foundational knowledge ensures that your short-term rental aligns seamlessly with local regulations, contributing to a smooth and lawful operation.

Property Type

Selecting the right property type is a pivotal decision in the success of your short-term rental venture. Consider the preferences of your target market when choosing between options such as apartments, houses, condos, or villas. Each property type attracts a distinct audience, and aligning your choice with the needs and expectations of your potential guests is essential. Moreover, assess the size and layout of the property, ensuring it caters to the comfort and convenience of your guests. A well-suited property type, coupled with thoughtful consideration of size and layout, enhances the overall appeal of your short-term rental and contributes to positive guest experiences.

Amenities and Features

Elevating the guest experience through thoughtful amenities and distinctive features is a key aspect of managing a successful short-term rental. Provide amenities beyond the basics, such as a fully equipped kitchen, Wi-Fi access, parking facilities, and laundry services, ensuring guests feel comfortable and accommodated. Additionally, consider incorporating unique features or themes that set your property apart from others. This could range from charming outdoor spaces to themed decor that resonates with your target audience. By offering a combination of essential conveniences and standout features, you meet modern travelers' expectations and create a memorable and appealing environment that encourages positive reviews and repeat bookings.

Condition and Maintenance

The condition and maintenance of your short-term rental property are pivotal factors in ensuring guest satisfaction and overall success. When selecting a property, opt for one in good condition or be prepared for necessary renovations to create a comfortable and appealing space. Regular maintenance is paramount to meet safety standards and guarantee a positive guest experience. Implementing a proactive maintenance schedule, addressing any issues promptly, and periodically updating the property contribute not only to the longevity of your investment but also to the trust and satisfaction of your guests. A well-maintained property not only attracts positive reviews but also establishes a reputation for reliability, encouraging repeat visits and positive word-of-mouth recommendations.

Scalability

When delving into short-term rentals, it's crucial to assess the potential for scalability. If your overarching goal involves expanding your rental business, strategic consideration of properties that offer scalability becomes paramount. Look for properties that can be easily replicated or managed efficiently, ensuring a seamless and sustainable growth trajectory. This involves not only choosing properties with universal appeal but also establishing standardized processes that can be applied across multiple locations. By proactively evaluating scalability, you set the foundation for a scalable and profitable short-term rental business that can adapt and thrive in evolving market conditions.

Budget Considerations

Budget considerations are at the forefront of establishing a successful short-term rental venture. It's imperative to meticulously establish a budget and maintain a realistic assessment of your financial capabilities from the outset. Take into account not only the purchase price of the property but also potential renovation costs, property taxes, insurance, and ongoing maintenance expenses. A transparent and comprehensive budgetary plan enables you to make informed decisions, avoid financial strain, and ensures the long-term viability of your short-term rental investment. By factoring in all associated costs, you create a solid financial foundation, allowing you to navigate challenges, seize opportunities for improvement, and ultimately maximize the profitability of your short-term rental property.

Regulatory Compliance

Adhering to regulatory compliance is non-negotiable in short-term rentals. It is imperative to ensure that your property aligns with local regulations and licensing requirements governing short-term rentals. Thoroughly familiarize yourself with any specific restrictions or guidelines imposed by homeowner associations or community rules, as these may have a direct impact on the operation of your rental property. By staying well-informed and in compliance with all pertinent regulations, you not only uphold ethical standards but also mitigate the risk of legal issues. This commitment to regulatory diligence not only fosters a responsible and sustainable short-term rental business but also builds trust with guests and surrounding communities, contributing to the overall success and longevity of your venture.

Potential for Year-Round Occupancy

When selecting a property for short-term rentals, it's crucial to assess its potential for year-round occupancy. Consider whether the property has the versatility to attract guests across different seasons or events. Properties located in areas with diverse attractions, catering to both summer and winter activities or near venues hosting year-round events, may offer consistent appeal. Understanding the property's seasonal demand patterns enables you to implement strategic pricing and marketing strategies, ensuring optimal occupancy throughout the year. A property with a year-round appeal not only maximizes revenue but also provides a stable and sustainable foundation for your short-term rental business.

Accessibility and Safety

Prioritizing accessibility and safety is paramount when managing a short-term rental property. It's crucial to ensure the property is safe and accessible, incorporating features such as proper lighting, secure entrances, and prominently displayed emergency information. Compliance with safety regulations is not only a legal requirement but also a fundamental commitment to the well-being of your guests. Provide clear and concise guidelines for guests to navigate the property safely and respond to emergencies effectively. By establishing a secure and accessible environment, you not only meet regulatory standards but also foster trust and confidence among your guests, contributing to a positive and memorable experience during their stay.

Neighborhood Dynamics

A comprehensive understanding of neighborhood dynamics is crucial for successfully managing a short-term rental. Consider factors such as noise levels, safety, and the community's overall attitude toward short-term rentals. By familiarizing yourself with the local environment, you can proactively address potential challenges and ensure a harmonious coexistence with neighbors. Building positive relationships with those in the community is key to mitigating any concerns and fostering open communication. This approach not only contributes to a peaceful living environment but also establishes your short-term rental as a responsible and considerate member of the neighborhood. By navigating and respecting neighborhood dynamics, you create a foundation for a thriving and well-integrated short-term rental business.

Market Competition

A thorough analysis of market competition is essential for positioning your short-term rental successfully. Take the time to scrutinize properties similar to yours in the area, identifying their strengths and weaknesses. By understanding the landscape, you can pinpoint opportunities to differentiate your property and offer unique value to potential guests. Whether through distinctive amenities, personalized services, or strategic pricing, finding ways to stand out in a competitive market enhances the appeal of your short-term rental. This proactive approach not only helps you cater to the specific needs and preferences of your target audience but also positions your property as a top choice amidst the competition, contributing to sustained success in the dynamic short-term rental market.

Technology Integration

Embracing technology integration is a pivotal strategy for elevating your short-term rental business. Explore incorporating smart home features to enhance guest experiences and streamline operations. Keyless entry systems, Wi-Fi connectivity, and other technological solutions can significantly improve convenience for your guests. Implementing these advancements not only caters to the modern traveler's expectations but also sets your property apart in a competitive market. The seamless integration of technology enhances security, accessibility, and overall satisfaction for your guests, contributing to positive reviews and repeat bookings. By staying at the forefront of technological trends, you position your short-term rental as a contemporary and accommodating choice, fostering a reputation for innovation and convenience in the hospitality landscape.

Selecting the right property for your short-term rental involves meticulously considering various factors. By aligning the property with market demand, ensuring legal compliance, and focusing on guest experience, you pave the way for a successful venture. Thorough research and, when necessary, seeking professional advice are paramount in making informed decisions. This approach not only enhances the property's appeal to potential guests but also establishes a solid foundation for sustainable and profitable operations in the dynamic landscape of short-term rentals.

6. Interior design tips to attract guests

Crafting an inviting and aesthetically pleasing interior is a key element in creating a memorable experience for guests at your short-term rental. The ambiance and visual appeal of the space play a significant role in attracting and retaining visitors. In this guide, we'll explore valuable interior design tips that go beyond mere decoration, aiming to elevate the overall atmosphere of your property and make it a sought-after destination for travelers. From strategic color schemes to thoughtful furniture arrangements, these tips are designed to enhance the appeal of your short-term rental and leave a lasting impression on every guest who walks through the door.

Neutral Color Palette

Opting for a neutral color palette in your short-term rental can significantly contribute to its overall charm and timeless appeal. Consider using neutral tones for walls and major furnishings, as these hues create a versatile and universally appealing backdrop. Neutrals such as whites, greys, and earthy tones not only exude a sense of sophistication but also provide a neutral canvas that allows for easy integration of various decor styles. This approach not only enhances the visual spaciousness of the space but also caters to a broad spectrum of guest preferences. A neutral color scheme sets the stage for a calming and welcoming atmosphere, ensuring that your short-term rental becomes a haven for relaxation and enjoyment for every guest.

Comfortable Furniture

Ensuring the comfort of your guests is paramount in creating a positive and inviting atmosphere in your short-term rental. Invest in comfortable and high-quality furniture to enhance the overall experience. Opt for durable materials that are not only aesthetically pleasing but also easy to clean, ensuring practicality and longevity. A mix of seating options, such as plush sofas, cozy armchairs, and versatile seating arrangements, caters to various preferences and encourages a sense of homeliness. By prioritizing comfort and quality in your furniture choices, you not only elevate the overall appeal of your space but also provide a welcoming environment that promotes relaxation and enjoyment for every guest during their stay.

Functional Layout

A functional layout is essential in maximizing the space and creating a harmonious environment in your short-term rental. Design to avoid clutter and ensure clear pathways, allowing guests to navigate the space effortlessly. Arrange furniture strategically to establish cozy and inviting seating areas, promoting a sense of comfort and relaxation. By thoughtfully planning the layout, you not only enhance the visual appeal of the space but also optimize its functionality. A well-organized and purposeful arrangement contributes to a positive guest experience, making the short-term rental a place where form seamlessly meets function.

High-Quality Bedding

Investing in high-quality bedding is a crucial element in ensuring a positive and restful experience for guests in your short-term rental. Opt for crisp linens, soft pillows, and a cozy duvet to create a welcoming and comfortable sleeping environment. Quality bedding not only enhances the overall aesthetics of the space but also contributes to a luxurious and enjoyable stay for your guests. Paying attention to details like the texture and cleanliness of the bedding adds a touch of sophistication, making the short-term rental feel like a home away from home. This commitment to providing top-notch sleeping amenities establishes your property as a desirable choice, fostering positive reviews and encouraging repeat bookings from satisfied guests.

Ample Storage

Offering ample storage options is a thoughtful consideration that enhances the functionality of your short-term rental. Provide guests with the convenience of unpacking and organizing their belongings by incorporating spacious closets, drawers, and shelving units. Utilize multi-functional furniture with built-in storage solutions to maximize space efficiency. This not only caters to the practical needs of your guests but also promotes a clutter-free and organized living space. A well-thought-out storage strategy adds to the overall comfort and convenience, contributing to a positive guest experience. By prioritizing ample storage, you create a welcoming environment that reflects your commitment to meeting the diverse needs of your guests during their stay.

Local Art and Decor

Infuse your short-term rental with local art and decor to imbue it with a unique and authentic ambiance. By incorporating pieces that reflect the cultural and aesthetic elements of the location, you create a space that tells a story and resonates with the local surroundings. Consider featuring artwork from local artists, indigenous crafts, or decorative items that showcase the region's distinctive character. This not only adds a personalized touch to your property but also offers guests a genuine and immersive experience. Local art and decor not only contribute to the visual appeal but also create a sense of connection with the destination, making the short-term rental a memorable and culturally rich retreat for your guests.

Well-Equipped Kitchen

A well-equipped kitchen is a fundamental component of a comfortable and enjoyable stay in a short-term rental. Ensure that your kitchen is stocked with essential appliances, quality cookware, and a comprehensive set of utensils. This not only facilitates a convenient cooking experience for guests but also enhances the overall functionality of the space. Consider going the extra mile by providing complimentary coffee, tea, and basic pantry items, offering a welcoming touch that adds to the guest experience. A thoughtfully equipped kitchen not only caters to the practical needs of your guests but also fosters a sense of homeliness, making your short-term rental a preferred choice for those seeking a home-away-from-home experience.

Smart Lighting

Embracing smart lighting solutions can significantly elevate the ambiance and functionality of your short-term rental. Installing smart lighting allows you to create various moods, from cozy and relaxing to vibrant and invigorating, enhancing the overall guest experience. Consider incorporating adjustable lamps and dimmers to provide flexibility in lighting levels, allowing guests to customize the ambiance according to their preferences. This not only adds a touch of modernity to your property but also offers practicality and convenience. Smart lighting contributes to creating a dynamic and comfortable atmosphere, making your short-term rental a contemporary and enjoyable space for guests to unwind and enjoy their stay.

Tech-Friendly Features

Incorporating tech-friendly features into your short-term rental enhances both convenience and modernity for your guests. Integrate smart thermostats, keyless entry systems, and high-speed Wi-Fi to streamline their experience. Smart thermostats offer climate control at their fingertips, keyless entry systems provide hassle-free access, and high-speed Wi-Fi caters to their connectivity needs. To ensure a smooth experience, provide clear and user-friendly instructions on how to use these tech amenities. By offering such contemporary conveniences, you not only cater to the preferences of tech-savvy travelers but also establish your short-term rental as a cutting-edge and welcoming space for a diverse range of guests.

Personalized Touches

Infusing personalized touches into your short-term rental is a thoughtful way to create a warm and welcoming atmosphere for your guests. Consider adding a welcome basket with local treats, providing guidebooks that showcase the best attractions in the area, or including a handwritten note expressing your appreciation for their stay. These personalized elements go beyond mere accommodation, making guests feel valued and cared for. Tailor these touches to cater to the preferences of your target audience, whether it's a family-friendly setup, a romantic retreat, or business-focused amenities. By incorporating these personal touches, you not only enhance the overall guest experience but also foster a connection that makes your short-term rental stand out as a memorable and considerate choice.

Greenery and Plants

Introducing greenery and plants into your short-term rental is a simple yet effective way to infuse a touch of nature and freshness into the space. Opt for low-maintenance indoor plants, adding vibrancy without requiring extensive care. Consider strategically placing these plants in areas that enhance the overall aesthetic and contribute to a positive atmosphere. Additionally, incorporating faux plants can be a practical choice for those looking to maintain the aesthetic appeal without the need for ongoing maintenance. The presence of greenery not only elevates the visual appeal of your rental property but also creates a calming and rejuvenating environment for guests during their stay.

Quality Flooring

Selecting quality flooring is a crucial aspect of creating a comfortable and visually appealing environment in your short-term rental. Opt for durable and easy-to-clean flooring options such as hardwood, laminate, or quality vinyl, combining style with practicality. These materials not only contribute to an elegant aesthetic but also ensure longevity and easy maintenance. To add warmth and texture to the space, incorporate rugs strategically placed in high-traffic areas. Consider including washable rugs like Ruggable for added convenience and easy cleaning between guest stays. By prioritizing quality flooring and thoughtful rug choices, you not only enhance the overall aesthetics of your short-term rental but also ensure a practical and inviting living space for your guests.

Quality Window Treatments

Investing in quality window treatments is essential for enhancing both the aesthetic and functional aspects of your short-term rental. Opt for curtains or blinds that not only complement the overall design of the space but also offer privacy and control over natural light. Consider including window treatments that open from both the top and bottom, providing versatility in adjusting light levels and maintaining privacy. Quality window treatments not only add a finishing touch to the decor but also contribute to the comfort and satisfaction of your guests. By prioritizing these elements, you create a well-appointed and stylish atmosphere in your short-term rental, ensuring that every guest enjoys a pleasant and customizable living space.

Themed Decor (If Appropriate)

Themed decor can be a captivating addition to your short-term rental, especially if your property is situated in a location with a distinct cultural or historical background. When considering a theme, aim for subtlety and cohesiveness to enhance the guest experience without overwhelming them. Choose elements that resonate with the local context, whether it's coastal motifs, historical references, or cultural symbols. Themed decor adds a unique charm to your rental property, creating a memorable and immersive stay for guests who appreciate the subtle integration of the local surroundings into their temporary home. Striking the right balance ensures that the themed decor contributes positively to the overall ambiance without becoming a dominant or distracting feature in the space.

Safety Features

Incorporating safety features into your short-term rental, such as smoke detectors, fire extinguishers, and easily accessible emergency information, is crucial for guest well-being. These measures contribute to a secure environment without compromising the aesthetic appeal of the space. Conceal safety devices within tasteful design elements or choose sleek, modern options that blend seamlessly with the decor. Additionally, consider utilizing monitored services for added security. Monitored smoke detectors and security systems can provide real-time alerts, enhancing overall safety. While prioritizing safety, integrating such monitored services ensures a proactive approach, offering peace of mind to both you and your guests during their stay in your short-term rental.

In conclusion, the design of your short-term rental space plays a pivotal role in attracting guests and fostering positive experiences that lead to glowing reviews and repeat bookings. A well-designed interior not only creates an inviting atmosphere but also leaves a lasting impression on guests. To uphold this standard, commit to regular updates and maintenance, ensuring that the space remains fresh and welcoming for every guest. By continuously investing in the aesthetics and functionality of your short-term rental, you not only meet the evolving expectations of your guests but also cultivate a reputation for providing exceptional stays, contributing to the ongoing success of your rental property.

7. Essential Amenities and Furnishings

Ensuring Guest Comfort and Convenience

Creating a memorable and enjoyable stay for short-term rental guests requires careful consideration of essential amenities and furnishings. Anticipating the needs and desires of your guests is key to providing a home-away-from-home experience. This chapter outlines the fundamental items that can elevate the overall guest experience in your short-term rental property, setting the foundation for comfort, convenience, and positive reviews.

Furniture

Comfortable seating in the living area.Dining table and chairs.Quality beds and bedroom furniture.

Bedding and Linens

High-quality sheets and pillowcases.
Comfortable pillows and duvets.
Spare bedding for longer stays.

Kitchen Essentials

Fully equipped kitchen with appliances (refrigerator, stove, oven, microwave).
Cookware, pots, and pans.
Dinnerware, glassware, and utensils.
Coffee maker, kettle, blender, and toaster.
Basic pantry items (coffee, tea, sugar, salt, pepper).

Toiletries

Towels (bath and hand towels).
Shampoo, conditioner, and body wash.
Toilet paper and tissues.
Hairdryer.

Cleaning Supplies

Cleaning products (all-purpose cleaner, dish soap).
Broom, mop, and vacuum cleaner.
Trash bags and recycling bins.

Technology and Entertainment

High-speed Wi-Fi.
Smart TV with streaming services.
Charging stations and adapters (these can be built into nightstands and tables).
Clear instructions for using tech amenities.

Safety and Security

Smoke and carbon monoxide detectors; monitoring services recommended.
Fire extinguisher.
First aid kit.
Emergency contact information.

Storage Solutions

Ample closet space with hangers.
Dresser or drawers for clothing storage.
Luggage racks.

Comfort Items

Blankets and throws for added comfort.
Extra pillows.
Heating or cooling options (fans, space heaters, or air conditioning).

Keyless Entry System

Implement a secure keyless entry system for easy check-in and check-out.

Bathroom Essentials

Hand soap and hand sanitizer.
Shower curtain.
Towel hooks or bars.

Outdoor Amenities

If applicable, outdoor furniture such as a patio set or balcony seating.
Grill or barbecue equipment.
Parking passes, Amenity passes.
Hot tub

Laundry Facilities

Washer and dryer or access to a laundry room.
Iron and ironing board.

Information and Guides

Welcome binder with essential information (Wi-Fi details, emergency contacts, local attractions).
Local guidebooks or recommendations.

Child-Friendly Items (if applicable)

Crib or playpen.Childproofing features.Kid-friendly dishes and utensils.

Personal Touches

Consider personal touches such as welcome notes or small welcome gifts.

Clear House Rules

Clearly outline house rules regarding smoking, pets, and other important guidelines.

Tailor these amenities and furnishings to your target audience and the unique features of your property. Regularly assess and update these items to ensure they remain in good condition and meet the needs of your guests. A well-equipped and thoughtfully furnished space contributes to a positive guest experience and can lead to positive reviews and repeat bookings.

8. Home maintenance and safety measures

Maintaining a safe and well-maintained short-term rental property is essential for guest satisfaction and compliance with regulations. Here are home maintenance and safety measures to consider for your short-term rental

Regular Inspections

Conduct regular inspections of the property to identify and address any maintenance issues.
Check for leaks, faulty appliances, and signs of wear and tear.

Professional Cleaning

Arrange professional cleaning services before each guest's arrival.
Ensure all surfaces, linens, and amenities are thoroughly cleaned and sanitized.

Safety Inspections

Periodically inspect safety features such as smoke detectors, carbon monoxide detectors, and fire extinguishers.
Replace batteries in detectors as needed.

Emergency Preparedness

Provide guests with clear instructions, including evacuation plans and emergency contact information.
Display emergency numbers for local services (fire, police, medical).

Secure Entry and Locks

Ensure all entry points, including windows and doors, are secure.
Implement a reliable keyless entry system for controlled access.

Routine Maintenance Tasks

Schedule routine maintenance tasks, including HVAC system checks,
plumbing inspections, and appliance maintenance.
Regularly service and clean essential systems to prevent breakdowns.

Adequate Lighting

Install adequate lighting in all areas of the property, both inside and
outside.
Check and replace light bulbs regularly.

Childproofing

If your property is family-friendly, consider implementing childproofing measures.
Cover electrical outlets, secure heavy furniture, and remove potential
hazards.

Property Exterior

Maintain the exterior, including landscaping and outdoor spaces.
Ensure pathways and outdoor areas are well-lit and safe.

Pest Control

Implement pest control measures to prevent infestations.
Regularly inspect for signs of pests and take appropriate action.

Regular Appliance Checks

Check and maintain appliances regularly to ensure they are in good working condition.
Replace or repair any malfunctioning appliances promptly.

Clear House Rules

Communicate house rules to guests, including safety and property maintenance guidelines.
Set expectations for guests' responsibilities in maintaining the property.

Secure Furnishings

Ensure all furnishings are secure and meet safety standards.
Regularly check for any loose or unstable furniture.

Accessibility Features

If your property accommodates guests with disabilities, ensure that accessibility features are well-maintained and functional.

Weather Preparedness

Secure outdoor furniture and equipment for adverse weather conditions. Provide necessary information to guests regarding weather-related precautions.

Regular Property Updates

Stay informed about changes to local regulations or safety standards. Implement necessary updates to meet current requirements.

By prioritizing home maintenance and safety measures, you enhance the overall guest experience and demonstrate your commitment to their well-being. Regular upkeep and a proactive approach to safety contribute to positive reviews and encourage repeat bookings.

3

Chapter 3: Setting the Right Price

9. Pricing Strategies for Maximum Profitability

Developing effective pricing strategies is essential for maximizing profitability in the short-term rental market. Here are several strategies to consider

Dynamic Pricing

Dynamic pricing is a strategic approach that involves adjusting the rates of short-term rental properties based on various factors such as demand, seasonality, local events, and booking lead time. By dynamically altering prices, hosts can optimize revenue and stay competitive in the market. During peak seasons or high-demand periods, prices may increase to reflect the heightened interest in accommodations. Conversely, during low-demand periods or last-minute bookings, prices may be adjusted downward to attract more guests. This flexible pricing strategy not only maximizes profitability for hosts but also provides guests with diverse pricing options, creating a win-win scenario in the dynamic landscape of short-term rentals.

Utilizing pricing tools or algorithms is a key element in optimizing the revenue of short-term rentals. These sophisticated tools enable hosts to automatically adjust rates in response to dynamic market conditions. By analyzing factors such as demand fluctuations, competitor pricing, and upcoming local events, these algorithms can make real-time adjustments to ensure that the property is priced competitively. This proactive approach not only saves hosts time but also allows for precise and data-driven decision-making. The use of pricing tools contributes to the efficiency of managing short-term rentals, ensuring that rates are always aligned with the current market scenario to maximize both occupancy and profitability.

Competitor Analysis

Regularly conducting a thorough competitor analysis is essential for short-term rental hosts seeking to optimize their pricing strategies. By closely examining competitors' pricing in the local area, hosts can gain valuable insights into market trends, demand fluctuations, and the competitive landscape. This analysis involves assessing not only the base rates but also any discounts, promotions, or unique offerings that competitors may have. Armed with this information, hosts can make informed decisions about adjusting their own pricing to remain competitive and attractive to potential guests. Staying vigilant through ongoing competitor analysis ensures that hosts are adaptable to changes in the market, allowing them to position their short-term rentals effectively and maintain a strong market presence.

In the dynamic landscape of short-term rentals, adapting to market conditions is crucial for hosts to stay competitive and attract guests. Adjusting rates is not just about being responsive to pricing trends but also about offering additional value to guests. By carefully analyzing the market and understanding guest preferences, hosts can strike a balance between competitive pricing and providing enhanced amenities, services, or unique experiences. This strategic approach not only keeps the property attractive in the eyes of potential guests but also contributes to building a positive reputation and fostering guest loyalty. By continually reassessing rates and adding value, hosts can create a win-win scenario, ensuring both competitiveness in the market and a memorable experience for their guests.

Seasonal Pricing

Seasonal pricing is a fundamental strategy in the short-term rental industry, allowing hosts to align rates with the varying demand throughout the year. During peak seasons when demand is high, such as holidays or local events, hosts can maximize revenue by increasing rates to reflect the heightened interest in accommodations. Conversely, during off-peak periods, adjusting rates downward can attract more guests and maintain consistent occupancy. This adaptive pricing model not only optimizes profitability but also ensures that the property remains competitive and attractive to potential guests regardless of the season. By strategically navigating the ebb and flow of demand, hosts can capitalize on the dynamic nature of the market and enhance the overall success of their short-term rental.

When setting seasonal prices for short-term rentals, it's crucial to consider a holistic approach that takes into account local events, holidays, and weather patterns. These factors play a significant role in influencing demand and can impact the attractiveness of a property to potential guests. For instance, during major local events or holidays, demand typically surges, allowing hosts to adjust prices accordingly to maximize revenue. Additionally, understanding regional weather patterns is essential, as certain seasons or weather conditions may draw more visitors. By incorporating these elements into the pricing strategy, hosts can not only stay competitive but also provide guests with a tailored experience that aligns with the unique aspects of the destination during different times of the year. This thoughtful approach contributes to both guest satisfaction and the overall success of the short-term rental.

Special Promotions

Implementing special promotions is a strategic tactic for short-term rental hosts looking to boost bookings and attract a wider audience. By offering promotions, discounts, or enticing package deals during specific periods, hosts can create a sense of urgency and incentivize potential guests to make reservations. These promotions could be aligned with off-peak seasons, local events, or holidays, providing an extra incentive for guests to choose a particular property over others. Special promotions not only stimulate demand during slower periods but also contribute to guest satisfaction and loyalty. This dynamic pricing approach allows hosts to tap into various market segments, optimize occupancy rates, and maintain a competitive edge in the ever-evolving landscape of short-term rentals.

Implementing promotional pricing for last-minute bookings or extended stays is a savvy strategy to optimize occupancy rates and cater to diverse guest needs. For last-minute bookings, offering discounted rates encourages spontaneous travelers to choose your property, helping to fill vacant dates and maximize revenue. Similarly, special pricing for extended stays appeals to guests seeking a more prolonged and cost-effective accommodation solution. This dynamic approach not only enhances the property's flexibility in meeting guest preferences but also contributes to overall guest satisfaction. By leveraging promotional pricing strategically, hosts can strike a balance between attracting a broad range of guests and ensuring the financial success of their short-term rental.

Length-of-Stay Discounts

Length-of-stay discounts present an effective strategy for short-term rental hosts aiming to incentivize longer bookings. By offering discounts for extended stays, hosts not only attract guests looking for a more prolonged experience but also maximize occupancy rates. This approach encourages guests to consider a more extended visit, promoting flexibility and affordability. Longer bookings contribute to a stable revenue stream for hosts while providing guests with cost-effective options, fostering a win-win scenario. The implementation of length-of-stay discounts reflects a host's commitment to accommodating the diverse needs of their guests and contributes to the overall success and appeal of the short-term rental property.

Implementing tiered pricing is a strategic approach to reward guests for booking longer durations in short-term rentals. This pricing model involves offering incremental discounts as the length of the stay increases. By providing financial incentives for extended bookings, hosts not only attract guests seeking a more extended experience but also foster loyalty and satisfaction. Tiered pricing communicates a host's appreciation for guests who choose a more prolonged stay, creating a mutually beneficial arrangement. This approach not only optimizes occupancy rates but also contributes to the overall positive reputation of the short-term rental, encouraging repeat bookings and establishing a robust relationship with guests.

Flexible Cancellation Policies

Offering flexible cancellation policies is a key strategy for short-term rental hosts seeking to attract more bookings and enhance guest confidence. A flexible cancellation policy provides guests with the assurance that they can adjust their plans without facing significant financial repercussions. In today's dynamic travel landscape, where uncertainties may arise, a flexible policy signals hosts' understanding and accommodation of guests' changing circumstances. This approach not only increases the appeal of the property to a broader range of potential guests but also contributes to a positive guest experience. By prioritizing flexibility, hosts build trust with guests, potentially leading to increased bookings, positive reviews, and enhanced overall success in the competitive short-term rental market.

Consideration of non-refundable bookings with lower rates is a strategic approach to encourage commitment from guests. By offering reduced rates for reservations with a non-refundable commitment, hosts not only attract guests who are certain about their travel plans but also minimize the impact of cancellations on their revenue. This pricing model provides an additional layer of flexibility for hosts to optimize occupancy and revenue, catering to a segment of travelers who prioritize cost savings and are confident in their travel arrangements. While appealing to budget-conscious guests, it also ensures a level of predictability for hosts, contributing to a more stable and secure short-term rental business.

Early Booking Discounts

Early booking discounts are a powerful incentive to encourage guests to secure their reservations well in advance. By offering discounts for early bookings, hosts create a sense of urgency and reward proactive guests who plan ahead. This strategy not only helps hosts secure bookings for future dates but also contributes to a more predictable and stable occupancy rate. Guests, in turn, benefit from cost savings and the assurance of securing their preferred accommodation. Early booking discounts not only stimulate demand during slower periods but also contribute to guest satisfaction and loyalty. This proactive approach enables hosts to optimize their short-term rental business and maintain a competitive edge in the ever-changing landscape of the hospitality industry.

Creating a sense of urgency through limited-time early booking offers is a dynamic strategy to drive prompt reservations for short-term rentals. By emphasizing the time-sensitive nature of these exclusive deals, hosts generate a heightened desire for potential guests to secure their accommodations promptly. Limited-time offers tap into the psychology of urgency, motivating travelers to make decisions quickly to avail themselves of the discounted rates. This approach not only stimulates demand during specific promotional periods but also instills a sense of excitement and anticipation among prospective guests. By strategically leveraging the concept of urgency in their marketing efforts, hosts can effectively boost early bookings, optimize occupancy rates, and enhance the overall success of their short-term rental business.

Utilize OTA Tools

To optimize pricing in the competitive landscape of short-term rentals, hosts can effectively utilize tools provided by online travel agencies (OTAs). These platforms often offer dynamic pricing tools and algorithms that take into account various factors such as demand, seasonality, local events, and competitor rates. By leveraging these OTA tools, hosts can automate the adjustment of their pricing strategy in real time, ensuring that rates remain competitive and responsive to market conditions. This approach not only streamlines the pricing process but also allows hosts to stay agile in the ever-changing hospitality industry. Additionally, utilizing OTA tools provides valuable insights into market trends and guest behavior, enabling hosts to make data-driven decisions for maximum profitability and success in the short-term rental market.

Harnessing the data and insights provided by online travel agencies (OTAs) is a strategic move for hosts looking to make informed decisions about their pricing strategy in the realm of short-term rentals. These platforms offer a wealth of information on market trends, guest preferences, and competitor pricing. By carefully analyzing this data, hosts can gain valuable insights into the ever-evolving dynamics of the hospitality industry. Understanding booking patterns, demand fluctuations, and seasonal trends allows hosts to adjust their pricing strategy with precision. This data-driven approach not only enhances the competitiveness of the short-term rental but also positions hosts to cater to the specific needs and expectations of their target audience. In essence, using OTA data empowers hosts to navigate the complexities of the market, ensuring a well-informed and adaptive pricing strategy that maximizes profitability.

Adjust Weekday vs. Weekend Rates

Adapting to demand patterns, hosts can strategically adjust weekday and weekend rates in their short-term rental pricing strategy. Recognizing that demand often varies between weekdays and weekends, hosts can set different rates to optimize revenue. Increasing rates for high-demand weekends, holidays, or special events capitalizes on peak periods when guests are willing to pay premium prices. Conversely, offering more competitive rates on weekdays may attract business travelers or guests seeking budget-friendly options during non-peak times. This nuanced approach not only reflects the dynamic nature of the market but also allows hosts to maximize profitability by aligning rates with specific demand trends, ensuring a well-balanced and responsive pricing strategy for their short-term rental.

Peak and Off-Peak Hours

Incorporating peak and off-peak pricing for specific hours of the day is a strategic move in optimizing short-term rental revenue. By charging higher rates for check-ins during peak arrival times, hosts can capitalize on periods of heightened demand when guests are more willing to pay a premium. This approach allows hosts to align their pricing strategy with the natural ebb and flow of guest activity, ensuring that rates reflect the value of the accommodation during peak hours. Simultaneously, offering lower rates during off-peak hours incentivizes guests who have flexibility in their check-in times. The implementation of peak and off-peak pricing not only maximizes revenue potential but also enhances the overall guest experience by providing tailored pricing options that cater to varying preferences and schedules.

Bundle Additional Services

A strategic approach to enhancing the value proposition of a short-term rental is to bundle additional services or amenities with the accommodation and adjust pricing accordingly. Hosts can consider including services such as cleaning fees, airport transfers, or special experiences as part of a comprehensive package. By bundling these extras, hosts not only streamline the booking process for guests but also create a more attractive and convenient offering. Adjusting pricing to reflect the bundled services ensures transparency and allows hosts to showcase the overall value guests receive. This approach not only increases the perceived value of the short-term rental but also provides an opportunity for hosts to differentiate their property in a competitive market while optimizing revenue by offering a customized and all-encompassing guest experience.

Regularly Review and Adjust

Success in the dynamic landscape of short-term rentals hinges on the proactive and continuous review of your pricing strategy. Regularly assessing performance metrics and staying abreast of changes in the local market dynamics enables hosts to make informed adjustments to their rates. Analyzing factors such as occupancy rates, guest reviews, and competitive pricing allows hosts to fine-tune their strategy for maximum profitability. Whether responding to shifts in demand, local events, or seasonal variations, the ability to adapt pricing accordingly is paramount. By embracing a data-driven approach and staying vigilant in monitoring market trends, hosts can ensure that their short-term rental remains competitive, attractive, and aligned with guest expectations, fostering sustained success in the ever-evolving world of hospitality.

Loyalty Programs

Fostering guest loyalty in the realm of short-term rentals can be achieved through the strategic implementation of loyalty programs. By introducing programs that reward repeat guests with exclusive discounts or perks, hosts can create a strong incentive for guests to choose their property for future stays. Offering special rates for subsequent bookings not only acknowledges and appreciates the loyalty of returning guests but also cultivates a sense of exclusivity. Loyalty programs not only contribute to guest retention but can also amplify positive word-of-mouth marketing, attracting new guests through the endorsement of satisfied repeat customers. This approach not only builds a community of loyal guests but also enhances the overall reputation and desirability of the short-term rental, creating a win-win scenario for both hosts and guests.

Monitor Guest Reviews

Guest reviews serve as invaluable feedback for hosts in the short-term rental business, providing insights into various aspects, including pricing. By closely monitoring reviews, hosts can gain a nuanced understanding of how guests perceive the value of their accommodation. Analyzing feedback related to pricing allows hosts to identify areas for improvement or adjustment in their pricing strategy. Addressing concerns or suggestions from guests not only demonstrates responsiveness but also contributes to an enhanced guest experience. The iterative process of refining the pricing strategy based on real-time guest feedback fosters continuous improvement, ensuring that the short-term rental remains competitive and aligns with the expectations of its target audience. Ultimately, the proactive integration of guest reviews into pricing decisions is a key component in maintaining guest satisfaction and optimizing the overall success of a short-term rental.

Consider Operating Costs

Setting the right pricing for a short-term rental necessitates a comprehensive consideration of all operating costs. Hosts should meticulously factor in expenses such as utilities, cleaning services, maintenance, and any property management fees when determining their rates. By ensuring that pricing accounts for all operational expenditures, hosts can guarantee the financial sustainability of their short-term rental venture. Striking a balance between covering costs and maintaining a reasonable profit margin is crucial for long-term success. A thorough understanding of the financial landscape, coupled with a transparent approach to pricing, ensures that hosts not only deliver value to guests but also run a sustainable and profitable operation in the competitive short-term rental market.

In the dynamic realm of short-term rentals, the key to sustained success lies in the ability to adapt and refine pricing strategies. By staying attuned to market dynamics, understanding guest preferences, and incorporating valuable feedback, hosts can fine-tune their pricing to remain competitive and maximize profitability. Regular reassessment and adjustments ensure a responsive approach to the evolving landscape of the industry, allowing hosts to optimize revenue streams and maintain a sustainable business model. In this ever-changing environment, the flexibility to adapt pricing strategies is a cornerstone for hosts seeking not only to meet but exceed guest expectations while achieving long-term success in the competitive short-term rental market.

10. Utilizing dynamic pricing tools

Utilizing dynamic pricing tools is a smart strategy for optimizing revenue in the short-term rental industry. These tools use algorithms and real-time data to adjust prices based on various factors. Here's how you can effectively use dynamic pricing tools for your short-term rental

Choose the Right Tool

Selecting the right dynamic pricing tool is a critical step in optimizing revenue for your short-term rental business. Thorough research is essential to identify a tool that aligns with your specific needs. Consider factors such as the tool's compatibility and ease of integration with your chosen booking platform, the range of features it offers, and feedback from other users. By carefully evaluating these aspects, you can make an informed decision that empowers you to implement a dynamic pricing strategy effectively. The right tool not only streamlines the pricing process but also enhances your ability to stay competitive and responsive in the ever-evolving landscape of the short-term rental market.

Understand Market Demand

To effectively utilize dynamic pricing tools, it is crucial to have a deep understanding of market demand in your specific area. These tools heavily rely on accurate and timely market demand data to make pricing adjustments. Factors such as local events, holidays, and seasonality play a significant role in influencing demand. Stay proactive in staying informed about upcoming events or trends that might impact the demand for short-term rentals. By keeping a finger on the pulse of local dynamics, you can align your pricing strategy with the ebb and flow of demand, ensuring that your rates remain competitive and responsive to the ever-changing market conditions.

Analyze Competitor Pricing

Leveraging dynamic pricing tools provides the opportunity to analyze competitor pricing in real-time, a crucial element in shaping a successful pricing strategy for short-term rentals. These tools enable hosts to stay abreast of their competitors' rates, allowing for nimble adjustments based on market dynamics. By understanding how other rentals in the vicinity are priced, hosts can position themselves competitively while considering factors like demand, amenities, and unique selling points. This proactive approach ensures that your pricing strategy is not only aligned with market demand but also takes into account your competitive position within the dynamic landscape of short-term rentals.

Optimize for Occupancy

To optimize occupancy rates in your short-term rental, it's essential to adjust pricing strategically. During low-demand periods, such as off-peak seasons or weekdays, consider implementing lower prices to attract more bookings. Experimentation with different price points is crucial to finding the sweet spot that maximizes bookings without compromising profitability. By dynamically adjusting pricing based on demand and carefully analyzing guest behavior, hosts can strike a balance that keeps their property consistently occupied, ensuring a steady flow of guests throughout the year. This approach not only fills gaps in the booking calendar during quieter times but also contributes to the overall success and financial viability of the short-term rental venture.

Set Minimum and Maximum Prices

Setting minimum and maximum price limits is a crucial aspect of an effective dynamic pricing strategy for short-term rentals. By establishing these limits, hosts can ensure that their pricing remains within acceptable ranges, taking into account factors such as the property's value, guest expectations, and local market conditions. The minimum price serves as a safeguard against underpricing, while the maximum price prevents overpricing that could deter potential guests. Striking the right balance between these limits allows hosts to adapt to market dynamics, optimize revenue, and maintain competitiveness in the ever-changing landscape of short-term rentals. Regularly reassessing and adjusting these limits based on market trends ensures a dynamic and effective pricing strategy.

Consider Lead Time

Considering lead time is a crucial component of a dynamic pricing strategy for short-term rentals. Dynamic pricing tools factor in the time between the booking date and the arrival date, allowing hosts to adjust prices accordingly. Offering discounts for last-minute bookings can help fill gaps in occupancy, attracting spontaneous travelers seeking immediate accommodation. On the other hand, incentivizing early bookings with lower rates encourages guests to plan in advance, providing hosts with a more predictable booking schedule. By fine-tuning prices based on lead time, hosts can optimize occupancy rates and revenue while catering to the diverse preferences of their guest demographic. Regularly monitoring and adjusting lead time strategies ensures flexibility and responsiveness to changing booking patterns.

Utilize Seasonal Adjustments

Seasonal adjustments are a key element of an effective dynamic pricing strategy for short-term rentals. By recognizing and adapting to fluctuations in demand throughout the year, hosts can optimize their pricing to reflect peak and off-peak seasons. During high-demand periods, such as holidays or local events, implementing higher prices maximizes revenue when demand is at its peak. Conversely, adjusting prices downward during slower seasons or off-peak times encourages bookings and ensures that the property remains competitive. This flexibility allows hosts to align their pricing with the ebb and flow of demand, ultimately maximizing occupancy and revenue across different seasons. Regularly reviewing and fine-tuning seasonal adjustments ensures that pricing remains responsive to market dynamics and guest preferences.

Monitor Local Events

Staying informed about local events, festivals, and conferences is crucial for optimizing your short-term rental pricing strategy. By keeping a close eye on the events calendar in your area, you can anticipate periods of increased demand for accommodations. Adjusting your pricing during peak demand associated with major events allows you to capitalize on the surge in visitors seeking accommodation. This proactive approach ensures that your rates align with the heightened demand, maximizing your property's revenue potential. Whether it's a popular festival, a major conference, or a significant local happening, tailoring your pricing to align with these events positions your short-term rental as an attractive and responsive option for guests during high-demand periods.

Customize for Weekdays and Weekends

Customizing your pricing strategy to differentiate between weekdays and weekends is a savvy approach in the dynamic landscape of short-term rentals. Recognizing that weekends or specific weekdays often witness heightened demand, hosts can strategically adjust prices to reflect this fluctuation. By setting distinct base prices for different days of the week, hosts can optimize revenue based on the varying preferences and behaviors of guests. This tailored approach allows hosts to maximize profits during peak demand periods while ensuring competitive and attractive rates during quieter times. Adapting pricing to the specific nuances of weekdays and weekends is a key element of a dynamic pricing strategy, contributing to increased bookings and overall profitability.

Factor in Minimum Stay Requirements

Incorporating minimum stay requirements into your dynamic pricing strategy is a strategic move to manage demand during peak seasons or special events. By setting minimum stay thresholds, hosts can encourage guests to book longer durations, ensuring a more stable occupancy and potentially reducing turnover costs. Adjusting pricing to incentivize extended stays not only aligns with the preferences of certain travelers but also contributes to a more efficient and profitable operation. This approach allows hosts to strike a balance between meeting guest expectations, maximizing occupancy, and optimizing revenue during periods of heightened demand.

Regularly Review and Adjust

To ensure the effectiveness of your dynamic pricing strategy, it's essential to conduct regular reviews and make adjustments accordingly. Keep a close eye on the performance of your pricing tool, assessing its impact on bookings, revenue, and overall competitiveness. Stay vigilant to changes in market conditions, including shifts in demand, local events, and competitor strategies. Regularly updating the parameters and settings of your dynamic pricing tool allows you to fine-tune your approach, ensuring it remains aligned with your business goals and the dynamic nature of the short-term rental market. By adopting a proactive stance and adapting your strategy as needed, you can maintain a competitive edge and optimize your revenue potential.

Stay Informed About Local Regulations

Staying informed about local regulations is crucial for the success of your dynamic pricing strategy. Familiarize yourself with any pricing regulations or restrictions imposed by local authorities to ensure compliance. Some areas may have specific guidelines regarding how pricing can be adjusted, and it's essential to operate within ethical boundaries. By staying informed about the legal landscape, you can mitigate the risk of any regulatory issues and build a pricing strategy that aligns with both market dynamics and local rules. This proactive approach not only safeguards your business but also fosters a positive relationship with the community and regulatory bodies.

Monitor Guest Reviews and Feedback

Monitoring guest reviews and feedback is a valuable practice to enhance your dynamic pricing strategy. Pay close attention to comments and observations about pricing from previous guests. Analyzing their feedback can provide valuable insights into whether your pricing strategy aligns with guest expectations and perceived value. If there are consistent mentions of pricing concerns or dissatisfaction, consider making adjustments to address these issues. By staying responsive to guest feedback, you not only improve the overall guest experience but also fine-tune your dynamic pricing approach to better meet the expectations of your target audience. This iterative process ensures that your pricing strategy remains dynamic and adaptable, contributing to positive guest experiences and sustained business success.

By incorporating dynamic pricing tools into your short-term rental strategy, you can optimize revenue, stay competitive, and adapt to changing market conditions. Regularly reassess and refine your pricing approach to ensure a balance between attracting bookings and maintaining profitability.

11. Special promotions and discounts

Implementing special promotions and discounts can be an effective strategy to attract more bookings, encourage more extended stays, and increase overall revenue for your short-term rental. Here are some special promotions and discount ideas

Early Booking Discounts

Implementing early booking discounts is a strategic approach to incentivize guests to make reservations well in advance. By offering a discount for early bookings, you create a sense of urgency, motivating potential guests to secure their stay ahead of time. This not only benefits guests by providing them with cost savings but also helps you secure bookings earlier, providing a clearer outlook on your property's occupancy. Early booking discounts can be promoted through various channels, such as your property listing or marketing campaigns, highlighting the value of planning ahead for both guests and your business.

Last-Minute Deals

Last-minute deals are an effective strategy to optimize occupancy and appeal to spontaneous travelers. By offering discounts for bookings made on short notice, you tap into a segment of the market that seeks flexibility and impromptu getaways. This approach helps maximize your property's utilization by filling last-minute vacancies, contributing to increased revenue and guest satisfaction. Promote these deals prominently on your booking platform and through targeted marketing channels to capture the attention of travelers looking for instant accommodation options. Last-minute deals not only benefit your business by minimizing unoccupied periods but also cater to the dynamic preferences of travelers seeking spontaneity in their travel plans.

Extended Stay Discounts

Extended stay discounts present a compelling incentive for guests seeking accommodation for an extended period. By offering reduced rates for bookings that surpass a specified duration, you cater to the needs of both business and leisure travelers. Business professionals on extended work assignments or families planning longer vacations often appreciate the cost savings associated with extended stay discounts. This strategy not only attracts guests looking for extended comfort but also contributes to a more stable and predictable booking schedule for your short-term rental. Highlight these discounts in your promotional materials and booking platform to attract guests considering prolonged stays, creating a win-win scenario for both hosts and guests.

Midweek Specials

Midweek specials serve as an effective strategy to increase occupancy during traditionally slower periods. By creating promotions specifically tailored for midweek stays, such as discounted rates for check-ins on weekdays, you can entice guests who might be more flexible with their travel dates. This approach not only helps fill gaps in your booking calendar but also attracts a demographic seeking more affordable options for their accommodation. Whether it's business travelers attending midweek conferences or leisure guests taking advantage of quieter weekdays, midweek specials provide an appealing incentive for potential guests, contributing to a more consistent and optimized booking flow for your short-term rental property. Highlight these promotions prominently in your marketing materials to capture the attention of guests looking for cost-effective midweek stays.

Seasonal Discounts

Seasonal discounts present a strategic approach to draw in more guests during specific seasons or events. By introducing promotions tailored to the unique characteristics of each season, such as summer getaways or holiday festivities, you can create added appeal for potential guests. Offering discounts during peak times not only attracts more bookings but also aligns with the preferences and expectations of travelers looking for cost-effective options during popular periods. Whether it's embracing the warmth of summer or celebrating festive occasions, seasonal discounts provide an opportunity to stand out in a competitive market and cater to the varied demands of your target audience. Ensure effective communication of these seasonal promotions through your marketing channels to capture the attention of guests planning their trips around specific times of the year.

Repeat Guest Discounts

A repeat guest discount program is a valuable strategy to cultivate guest loyalty and encourage recurring bookings. By recognizing and rewarding guests who choose your short-term rental repeatedly, you not only foster a sense of appreciation but also create a strong incentive for them to return. Consider offering exclusive discounts or personalized perks to repeat guests, acknowledging their commitment to your property. This not only enhances the guest experience but also contributes to positive reviews and recommendations. Implementing a well-designed loyalty program showcases your dedication to building lasting relationships with guests, ultimately contributing to the overall success and sustainability of your short-term rental business.

Referral Discounts

Introducing a referral discount program is an effective way to leverage the power of word-of-mouth marketing and expand your short-term rental network. By incentivizing guests to refer your property to their friends and family, you tap into a trusted channel for potential bookings. Offering discounts not only motivates your current guests to share their positive experiences but also attracts new guests who come with a recommendation. This mutually beneficial system fosters a sense of community around your property and can significantly contribute to a steady stream of bookings. Implementing a referral discount initiative is a strategic move to amplify your property's visibility and enhance its appeal among a broader audience.

Bundle Packages

Crafting bundled packages for your short-term rental can add value to the guest experience and attract bookings seeking an all-inclusive stay. By combining the accommodation with extra services or amenities such as airport transfers, guided tours, or spa services, you create a convenient and appealing proposition for guests. Offering these bundled packages at a discounted rate encourages guests to take advantage of the added services, enhancing their overall stay. This strategy not only increases the perceived value of your property but also sets it apart in a competitive market, catering to guests looking for a comprehensive and hassle-free experience. By carefully curating packages that align with your target audience's preferences, you create a compelling offering that can boost bookings and elevate the guest experience.

Off-Peak Specials

Introducing off-peak specials for your short-term rental during low-demand seasons is a strategic approach to boost bookings and maximize occupancy. By offering special discounts during periods when demand is typically lower, you create an incentive for guests to choose your property over others. This can help balance out seasonal variations, ensuring a more consistent flow of guests throughout the year. Tailoring these off-peak specials to align with the preferences and interests of your target audience can further enhance their appeal. Whether it's discounted rates, complimentary amenities, or other enticing offers, these specials not only attract cost-conscious travelers but also contribute to a positive guest experience. Embracing off-peak specials as part of your pricing strategy demonstrates flexibility and adaptability, ultimately contributing to the overall success of your short-term rental.

Social Media Promotions

Leveraging social media promotions is a dynamic strategy to directly engage with your audience and drive bookings for your short-term rental. By running exclusive promotions on platforms such as Instagram, Facebook, or Twitter, you can create a sense of urgency and excitement among your followers. Consider offering limited-time discounts, special packages, or unique perks for guests who book directly through your social media channels. This not only fosters a sense of community but also provides a direct and interactive channel for potential guests to access enticing offers. Additionally, social media promotions can enhance brand visibility, attract new followers, and generate buzz around your short-term rental business. Embrace the power of social media to not only showcase the charm of your property but also to strategically market promotions that capture the attention and interest of your target audience.

Flash Sales

Implementing flash sales is an effective strategy to infuse excitement and urgency into your short-term rental marketing. By offering significant discounts for a limited time, you can create a sense of urgency, prompting potential guests to make quick decisions and secure bookings. Flash sales are particularly impactful during specific periods, such as holidays, special events, or low-demand seasons, where the prospect of exclusive discounts can captivate your audience's attention. Utilize various marketing channels, including your website, social media, and email newsletters, to promote these flash sales and maximize their reach. This not only stimulates immediate bookings but also cultivates a dynamic and engaging relationship with your audience, encouraging repeat business and positive word-of-mouth referrals.

Group Discounts

Group discounts can be a compelling incentive to attract larger bookings and cater to the needs of groups traveling together. By offering discounts for reservations that accommodate a specified number of guests, you not only encourage the booking of multiple accommodations but also enhance the overall value proposition for group travelers. This strategy is particularly effective for properties with ample space and amenities suitable for larger gatherings. Highlight the advantages of booking as a group, such as shared expenses and a more communal experience, and ensure that your property can comfortably accommodate the number of guests specified in the discount offer. Group discounts contribute to expanding your customer base, fostering positive group experiences, and establishing your property as an accommodating choice for various travel purposes.

Special Events Promotions

Crafting special events promotions tailored to local festivities, festivals, or holidays can significantly boost bookings during specific periods. Aligning your promotional strategy with noteworthy events in your area allows you to tap into increased demand and attract guests seeking accommodations for these occasions. Consider offering event-specific discounts, packages, or perks to entice potential guests. Leverage the unique features of your property that align with the nature of the event, whether it's proximity to festivities, thematic decorations, or exclusive access to related experiences. By integrating your short-term rental into the local event scene, you not only enhance the overall guest experience but also position your property as a sought-after choice for those looking to make the most of special occasions. This targeted approach adds a layer of relevance and appeal, contributing to heightened visibility and increased bookings during event-driven periods.

Flexible Cancellation Discounts

Providing flexible cancellation discounts is a strategic approach to accommodate varying guest needs. By offering discounts for bookings with flexible cancellation policies, guests are more likely to feel confident in making reservations, knowing they have the flexibility to adjust their plans if needed. This not only enhances the guest experience but also serves as an attractive feature that can positively impact your property's booking rates. The ability to adapt to guests' preferences in terms of cancellation contributes to building trust and fostering a positive relationship between hosts and guests.

Package Deals for Special Occasions

Offering package deals for special occasions is a thoughtful way to enhance the overall guest experience. By curating special packages for events like birthdays, anniversaries, or holidays, hosts can provide guests with a memorable and celebratory stay. These packages may include personalized decorations, complimentary services, and discounted rates, creating a unique and festive atmosphere for guests during significant moments. Such tailored offerings not only add value to the guest's experience but also contribute to positive reviews and the likelihood of repeat bookings. By catering to special occasions, hosts can differentiate their property and create a lasting impression for guests celebrating important milestones.

Collaborate with Local Businesses

Collaborating with local businesses can be a strategic move to enhance the guest experience and provide added value to your short-term rental offerings. By partnering with nearby restaurants, spas, or attractions, hosts can create exclusive discounts or packages for their guests. This collaboration not only supports the local community but also offers guests convenient access to nearby amenities and experiences. Guests appreciate exploring the area and enjoying special perks, making their stay more enjoyable and memorable. Additionally, such collaborations can foster positive relationships with local businesses, potentially leading to mutual referrals and a stronger sense of community within the neighborhood.

First-Time Guest Discount

Introducing first-time guest discounts is a strategic approach to attracting new visitors and creating a positive impression of your short-term rental. By offering exclusive discounts to guests staying for the first time, you not only incentivize them to choose your property but also increase the likelihood of turning them into repeat customers. This promotional strategy can be highlighted in your marketing efforts, enticing potential guests who may be exploring various accommodation options. The discounted rates for first-time guests serve as a welcoming gesture, fostering a sense of hospitality and encouraging positive reviews. As a result, this approach can contribute to building a loyal customer base and enhancing the overall success of your short-term rental business.

Bundle Cleaning Fees

Opting to bundle cleaning fees into the nightly rate for specific periods can be an attractive strategy for guests seeking a transparent and simplified pricing structure. By incorporating cleaning fees within the overall rate, guests may perceive it as a more convenient and cost-effective option, eliminating the need to calculate additional expenses. This approach aligns with the trend of transparent pricing, enhancing the overall guest experience. Moreover, it can contribute to a smoother booking process, reducing the perceived financial burden associated with separate cleaning fees. As a host, bundling cleaning fees allows you to present a more straightforward and appealing pricing model, potentially increasing bookings and guest satisfaction.

When implementing promotions and discounts, you must consider your target audience, market trends, and the specific goals you aim to achieve. Regularly evaluate the performance of your promotions and adjust them based on guest feedback and booking patterns.

4

Chapter 4: Effective Marketing Strategies

13. Building a Compelling Online Listing

Building a compelling online listing is essential for attracting potential guests to your short-term rental. A well-crafted listing showcases your property and persuades potential guests to book. Here's a guide on how to build a compelling online listing

High-Quality Photos

Include high-resolution photos that showcase the key features of your property.

Capture different angles of rooms, amenities, and any unique aspects.

Detailed Property Description

Write a detailed and engaging property description highlighting key features, amenities, and the overall experience.

Use descriptive language to paint a vivid picture of the property.

Unique Selling Points

Identify and emphasize the unique selling points of your property.

Highlight any special features, views, or amenities that set your rental apart.

Clear and Concise Headline

Craft a clear and concise headline that encapsulates the essence of your property.

Use attention-grabbing language to capture potential guests' interest.

Highlight Amenities

Create a dedicated section highlighting available amenities.

Mention features like Wi-Fi, parking, kitchen facilities, and extras like a pool or outdoor space.

Provide House Rules

Clearly outline house rules to set expectations for guests.

Include rules on smoking, pets, check-in/out times, and other important guidelines.

Accurate Location Information

Provide accurate and detailed location information.

Include proximity to attractions, public transportation, and local amenities.

Transparent Pricing

Display pricing information, including additional fees (cleaning, taxes).

Be transparent about cancellation policies.

Interactive Floor Plan

If possible, include an interactive floor plan to help guests visualize the property's layout.

Guest Reviews and Testimonials

Encourage positive reviews from previous guests.

Display guest testimonials to build trust and credibility.

Respond to Questions Promptly

Be responsive to inquiries and questions from potential guests.

Promptly address queries to provide excellent customer service.

Local Recommendations

Include recommendations for local attractions, restaurants, and activities.

Provide a guidebook or links to nearby points of interest.

Professional Copywriting

Invest in professional copywriting to ensure your property description is compelling and well-written.

Use persuasive language to evoke a sense of experience and comfort.

Seasonal Content Updates

Update your listing with seasonal content and promotions.

Highlight any special offers or events happening during specific seasons.

Multilingual Listings

Consider creating multilingual listings to attract a diverse range of guests.

Translate key information to cater to an international audience.

Virtual Tour or Video Walkthrough

Provide a virtual tour or video walkthrough to give potential guests a comprehensive view of your property.

Instant Booking Option

If possible, enable the instant booking option to streamline the reservation process.

Many guests prefer the convenience of instant booking.

Engage with Professional Photographers

Consider hiring a professional photographer to capture the best images of your property.

Professional photos can significantly enhance the appeal of your listing.

Regularly Update Information

Keep your listing up to date with accurate information.

Update photos, amenities, and any changes to the property promptly.

Creating a compelling online listing requires attention to detail and a focus on providing potential guests with the information they need to make an informed decision. You increase the likelihood of attracting and booking guests by showcasing your property effectively and offering a positive online experience.

14. Utilizing professional photography

Utilizing professional photography for short-term rentals is a crucial invest-ment that can significantly enhance the appeal of your property and attract more bookings. Here's a guide on how to make the most of professional photography for your short-term rental

Hire a Professional Photographer

Invest in a skilled and experienced professional photographer specializ-ing in real estate or architectural photography.

Look for a photographer who understands the unique requirements of short-term rental listings.

Showcase Key Features

Work with the photographer to highlight the key features of your property.

Capture important areas such as bedrooms, living spaces, kitchens, and unique amenities.

Capture Different Angles

Ensure that the photographer captures various angles of each room to provide a comprehensive view.

Include shots from corners, doorways, and windows to showcase the layout effectively.

Pay Attention to Lighting

Schedule the photo shoot during optimal natural lighting conditions.

Ensure that each room is well-lit, and use artificial lighting strategically to enhance visibility.

Highlight Exterior Spaces

If your property has outdoor spaces, ensure they are well-documented. Capture images of gardens, balconies, patios, or any other outdoor features.

Emphasize Amenities

Showcase amenities such as a pool, gym, or outdoor seating through high-quality images.

Highlight any unique features that set your property apart.

Use High-Resolution Images

Ensure the photographer provides high-resolution images suitable for online listings.

High-quality images contribute to a professional and inviting presentation.

Capture Details

Encourage the photographer to capture details that make your property stand out, such as stylish decor, artwork, or architectural elements.

Virtual Tours or Video Walkthroughs

Consider including virtual tours or video walkthroughs in addition to static images.

Virtual tours provide an immersive experience and can enhance the online listing.

Edit Images Professionally

Invest in professional image editing to enhance colors, correct lighting, and ensure a polished look.

Eliminate any distracting elements or imperfections from the photos.

Consistent Branding

Maintain consistency in the visual style across all your images to establish a cohesive and branded look.

Consistent branding helps create a professional and trustworthy image.

Seasonal Updates

Consider updating your images seasonally to showcase the property in different settings.

Seasonal updates keep your listing fresh and relevant throughout the year.

Capture Lifestyle Shots

Include lifestyle shots that portray the experience guests can expect.

Show images of people enjoying the space, relaxing indoors or engaging in outdoor activities.

Highlight Local Attractions

If your property is located near attractions or landmarks, include images highlighting the area.

Showcase the neighborhood to add value to your listing.

Professional Editing Software

Use professional editing software to fine-tune images and ensure a consistent and polished appearance.

Editing tools can enhance colors, sharpness, and overall visual appeal.

Use Images Across Platforms

Utilize professional images in your online listing and across various marketing platforms, including your website and social media.

Investing in professional photography for your short-term rental is a valuable step toward creating an enticing and visually appealing listing. Quality images attract potential guests and convey unique features and ambiance.

15. Social media promotion and advertising

Leveraging social media promotion and advertising is a powerful strategy for increasing visibility, attracting potential guests, and driving bookings for your short-term rental. Here's a guide on effectively using social media to promote your short-term rental

Choose the Right Platforms

Identify the social media platforms that align with your target audience. Instagram, Facebook, and Pinterest are popular choices for travel and accommodation promotions.

Create Engaging Content

Develop high-quality, visually appealing content showcasing your property.

Include a mix of images, videos, and engaging captions that highlight the unique features and experiences your rental offers.

Build a Social Media Presence

Establish and maintain an active presence on chosen social media platforms.

Regularly post updates, share local insights, and interact with your audience to build a community around your rental.

Utilize Instagram Stories and Reels

Use Instagram Stories and Reels to share behind-the-scenes glimpses, virtual tours, and quick highlights.

These features offer a dynamic and engaging way to showcase your property.

Run Paid Advertising Campaigns

Invest in paid advertising on social media platforms to reach a larger audience.

Use targeted ads to reach specific demographics, interests, and geographical locations.

Collaborate with Influencers

Partner with local influencers or travel bloggers who align with your property's style and target audience.

Influencers can provide authentic reviews and promote your short-term rental to their followers.

Promote Special Offers and Discounts

Use social media to announce and promote special offers, discounts, or exclusive deals.

Create a sense of urgency to encourage followers to take immediate action.

Showcase Guest Experiences

Encourage guests to share their experiences on social media and use a branded hashtag.

Share user-generated content to build credibility and showcase the positive experiences of past guests.

Engage with Your Audience

Respond promptly to comments, messages, and inquiries.

Engage with your audience by asking questions, conducting polls, and encouraging feedback.

Utilize Facebook Marketplace

List your short-term rental on Facebook Marketplace to reach users actively searching for accommodation.

Ensure that your listing is detailed and images are visually appealing.

Create Facebook and Instagram Ads

Design visually striking ads that showcase your property for both Facebook and Instagram.

Use compelling copy and clear calls to action to drive traffic to your booking platform.

Utilize Pinterest for Inspirational Content

Create visually appealing pins on Pinterest that highlight your property's aesthetics, local attractions, and travel tips.

Utilize Pinterest boards to curate content that inspires potential guests.

Implement Geo-Targeting

Utilize geo-targeting in social media advertising to reach users in specific locations relevant to your property.

This is particularly effective for attracting local and regional guests.

Monitor Analytics and Metrics

Regularly monitor analytics and metrics provided by social media platforms.

Analyze the performance of your posts, ads, and engagement to refine your strategy.

Encourage Direct Bookings

Include a clear call-to-action in your social media posts and ads that direct users to your booking platform.

Encourage direct bookings by offering exclusive discounts or perks for those who book through social media channels.

Share Local Recommendations

Share recommendations for local attractions, restaurants, and activities to provide added value to your followers.

Position your property as a gateway to a unique and enjoyable travel experience.

Utilize Instagram IGTV for Longer Content

Use Instagram IGTV to share longer videos, such as property tours, interviews with staff, or in-depth guides about the local area.

By effectively utilizing social media promotion and advertising, you can increase the visibility of your short-term rental, engage with potential guests, and drive bookings. Stay consistent, adapt your strategy based on analytics, and build a robust online presence to attract a steady stream of guests.

16. Building a brand for your short-term rental

Building a solid brand for your short-term rental is essential for creating a unique identity, attracting guests, and fostering loyalty. Here's a comprehensive guide on how to build a brand for your short-term rental

Define Your Brand Identity

Clearly define your brand identity by identifying your property's unique features, values, and the experience you aim to provide.

Consider what sets your rental apart from others regarding style, amenities, and location.

Choose a Memorable Name and Logo

Select a memorable and distinctive name for your short-term rental.
Design a professional logo that reflects your property's personality and aligns with your brand identity.

Develop a Brand Story

Craft a compelling brand story that narrates your short-term rental's history, vision, and values.

Share your story on your website, social media, and other marketing materials.

Create a Consistent Visual Identity

Establish a consistent visual identity across all marketing channels.

Use a consistent color scheme, fonts, and imagery in your logo, website, and promotional materials.

Design a Professional Website

Create a professional and user-friendly website that showcases your property and brand.

Ensure the website is visually appealing, easy to navigate, and provides essential information for potential guests.

Utilize Professional Photography

Invest in professional photography to visually represent your property on your website and across marketing channels.

Use high-quality images that highlight your short-term rental's unique features and atmosphere.

Craft a Unique Selling Proposition (USP)

Clearly articulate your Unique Selling Proposition (USP) – what makes your rental stand out.

Communicate this USP consistently in your marketing materials and messaging.

Develop a Brand Voice

Define a voice that aligns with your property's personality and resonates with your target audience.

Use this voice in all written communication, including website content, social media posts, and guest communications.

Showcase Guest Testimonials

Feature positive guest testimonials and reviews prominently on your website and marketing materials.

Encourage guests to share their experiences and feedback on review platforms and social media.

Implement Consistent Branding Across Platforms

Ensure that your branding is consistent across various platforms, including online travel agencies (OTAs), social media, and third-party booking sites.

Maintain a cohesive brand image to build recognition.

Engage in Local Community Outreach

Engage with the local community to strengthen your ties and enhance your property's image.

Sponsor local events, collaborate with nearby businesses, or participate in community initiatives.

Create a Brand Guide

Develop a brand guide that outlines your brand elements, including logo usage, color palette, and typography.

Share this guide with staff and partners to maintain a cohesive brand image.

Offer Consistent Guest Experiences

Ensure that the guest experience aligns with your brand promise.

Consistency in service, cleanliness, and amenities builds trust and reinforces your brand.

Utilize Social Media Strategically

Leverage social media platforms to promote your brand and engage with your audience.

Share visually appealing content, promotions, and local insights reinforcing your brand identity.

Develop Promotional Materials

Create promotional materials, such as brochures, business cards, and branded stationery, that reflect your brand identity.

Use these materials for both online and offline marketing efforts.

Offer Branded Amenities

Consider offering branded amenities or merchandise (e.g., towels, robes, mugs) that guests can purchase or use during their stay.

Branded items serve as both souvenirs and promotional tools.

Stay Responsive and Engaged

Stay responsive to guest inquiries and feedback.

Engage with your audience on social media, respond to reviews, and address concerns promptly to build a positive brand reputation.

Monitor and Adapt

Regularly monitor your brand's performance across various channels.

Be open to feedback and adapt your branding strategy based on market trends and guest preferences.

Building a brand for your short-term rental takes time, consistency, and a deep understanding of your target audience. By developing a strong brand identity, maintaining consistency in your messaging and visuals, and delivering exceptional guest experiences, you can establish a reputable and recognizable brand that attracts and retains guests.

5

Chapter 5: Guest Experience and Satisfaction

17. Providing exceptional customer service

Providing exceptional customer service for your short-term rental is crucial for guest satisfaction, positive reviews, and repeat bookings. Here's a comprehensive guide on delivering outstanding customer service

Clear Communication

Establish clear communication channels with guests from the booking process through check-out.

Respond promptly to inquiries, provide detailed information, and set clear expectations.

Responsive Booking Process

Streamline the booking process to be user-friendly and efficient.

Use an easy-to-navigate website and booking platform and ensure a smooth reservation process.

Welcome Guests Warmly

Welcome guests warmly upon arrival.

Provide a personalized welcome message, a welcome kit, or a small gesture like a welcome drink.

Provide Detailed Information

Offer comprehensive information about the property, amenities, and local area in a guest handbook or through digital means.

Include emergency contact details and any specific instructions.

Be Proactive

Anticipate guests' needs and address potential concerns proactively.

Provide information on nearby services, attractions, and activities.

Personalized Guest Experience

Personalize the guest experience by remembering special occasions, preferences, or reasons for the stay.

Consider leaving a personal note or a small welcome gift based on guest information.

Quality Housekeeping

Ensure high standards of cleanliness and maintenance.

Regularly inspect the property to address any issues promptly.

Quick Resolution of Issues

Address any issues or concerns guests raise promptly and efficiently.

Offer solutions and compensate when necessary to ensure guest satisfaction.

Concierge Services

Provide concierge services or recommendations for local attractions, restaurants, and activities.

Assist with booking reservations or arranging transportation if possible.

Flexibility with Requests

Be flexible and accommodating with reasonable guest requests.

Consider early check-ins, late check-outs, or other requests when feasible.

24/7 Availability

Provide 24/7 availability for emergencies or urgent matters. -

Have a reliable contact method for guests to reach you anytime.

Collect Feedback

Encourage guests to provide feedback through reviews or surveys.

Use feedback to identify areas for improvement and showcase positive reviews on your website.

Implement Guest Recognition Programs

Implement guest recognition programs or loyalty programs to reward repeat guests.

Offer special discounts, perks, or exclusive offers to returning customers.

Training for Staff

If you have staff or property managers, ensure they are well-trained in customer service.

Provide guidelines on handling guest interactions and resolving issues.

Regular Property Inspections

Conduct regular inspections to identify and address maintenance or safety concerns.

Proactively manage and maintain the property to prevent issues during guest stays.

Offer Amenities and Extras

Provide thoughtful amenities and extras to enhance the guest experience.

This could include complimentary snacks, toiletries, or access to additional services.

Sustainable Practices

Implement sustainable practices in your property, such as recycling options or energy-efficient measures.

Communicate your commitment to sustainability, appealing to environmentally conscious guests.

Stay Informed About Local Events

Stay informed about local events, festivals, or changes in local regulations that may impact guests.

Provide timely information to guests to enhance their stay.

Social Media Engagement

Engage with guests on social media platforms.

Respond to comments, share positive reviews, and use social media to enhance your brand's customer service image.

Continuous Improvement

Regularly review and evaluate your customer service processes.

Identify areas for improvement and implement changes to enhance the overall guest experience.

Exceptional customer service is a critical differentiator in the short-term rental industry. By prioritizing guest satisfaction, maintaining clear communication, and continuously seeking ways to improve, you can create a positive and memorable experience for your guests, leading to positive reviews and repeat business.

18. Guest communication and expectations

Effective guest communication and clear expectations are crucial to managing a successful short-term rental. Here's a guide on handling guest communication and establishing expectations

Pre-Arrival Communication

Send a welcoming message to guests before their arrival, providing essential details such as check-in instructions, parking information, and contact numbers.

Include any specific details about the property or nearby attractions.

Provide Detailed Check-In Information

Clearly outline the check-in process, including key or lockbox instructions.

Include any necessary access codes and ensure guests have all the information they need to arrive smoothly.

Set Expectations Early

Communicate house rules, expectations, and specific policies before guests arrive.

Include information on check-out procedures and any penalties for non-compliance.

Guest Handbook or Welcome Kit

Create a guest handbook or welcome kit that includes essential information about the property, local attractions, emergency contact numbers, and any specific instructions.

Include recommendations for nearby restaurants, shops, and activities.

Be Responsive to Inquiries

Respond promptly to guest inquiries, whether they are sent via email, messaging platforms, or phone calls.

Address questions or concerns promptly.

Use a Clear Booking Platform

If you're using a booking platform, ensure that your property listing provides accurate and detailed information about the amenities, house rules, and check-in/check-out procedures.

Set clear expectations through the platform's messaging system.

Clear House Rules

Communicate house rules, including policies on smoking, pets, noise, and any other important guidelines.

Make sure guests understand the consequences of not following the rules.

Emergency Information

Provide emergency information, including the location of fire extinguishers, emergency exits, and contact details for local emergency services.

Communicate the procedures to follow in case of emergencies.

Regular Check-Ins During the Stay

Check-in with guests during their stay to ensure they have everything they need and address any concerns.

This can be done through messaging platforms, emails, or in-person visits.

Offer Assistance

Let guests know you're available to assist them with any questions or issues during their stay.

Provide contact information and response times.

Post-Stay Feedback

Encourage guests to provide feedback after their stay.

Use this feedback to improve your property and services for future guests.

Notify About Local Events

Inform guests about any local events, festivals, or construction projects that might impact their stay.

Manage expectations regarding potential noise or disruptions.

WiFi and Technology Information

Provide information about WiFi access, passwords, and any other technological features in the property.

Ensure that guests know how to operate devices and systems.

Check-Out Procedures

Communicate check-out procedures, including any requirements for cleaning, returning keys, or handling trash.

Specify the check-out time and any penalties for late check-out.

Address Guest Concerns Proactively

If guests express concerns or issues, address them proactively and promptly.

Offer solutions and ensure that guests feel heard and valued.

Local Transportation Information

Provide information about local transportation options, including public transit, taxi services, or car rental recommendations.

Cultural Considerations

If your property is in a culturally diverse area, provide information about local customs and cultural considerations.

This can enhance the guest experience and prevent misunderstandings.

Accessibility Information

Communicate information about the accessibility of your property, including the presence of stairs, ramps, or other features.

Ensure that guests with specific needs know the property's suitability.

Use Automation for Reminders

Use automation tools or booking platforms to send automated reminders about check-in details, house rules, and check-out procedures.

This helps reinforce important information.

Express Gratitude

Express gratitude to guests for choosing your property.

A thank-you note or small gesture upon arrival can set a positive tone for the stay.

Effective communication and clear expectations contribute significantly to a positive guest experience. Providing thorough information, being responsive, and proactively addressing concerns can create a seamless and enjoyable stay for your short-term rental guests.

19. Tips for creating memorable experiences

Creating memorable experiences for guests in your short-term rental can lead to positive reviews, repeat bookings, and enthusiastic recommendations. Here are tips to make your short-term rental stand out and provide unforgettable experiences

Personalized Welcome

Provide a personalized welcome for guests. This could include a welcome note, a small gift, or local treats that add a personal touch to their arrival.

Thoughtful Amenities

Offer thoughtful amenities that enhance the guest experience. This could include high-quality toiletries, extra linens, a well-stocked kitchen, or even bicycles for exploring the area.

Local Recommendations

Provide a curated list of local recommendations for restaurants, attractions, and activities. Tailor suggestions to the interests of your guests and include insider tips.

Welcome Guide or Handbook

Create a comprehensive welcome guide or handbook with all essential information about the property, nearby attractions, emergency contacts, and house rules.

Ambiance to create a memorable atmosphere for guests.

Special Occasion Celebrations

Celebrate special occasions with guests, such as birthdays or anniversaries. Consider leaving a small surprise or arranging for local services like flowers or a special meal.

Events and Workshops

Host events or workshops for guests, such as cooking classes, local craft sessions, or guided tours. This creates an opportunity for guests to connect and enjoy unique experiences.

Outdoor Experiences

If applicable, enhance outdoor spaces. Create a cozy patio, provide outdoor games, or set up a barbecue area for guests to enjoy the outdoors.

Engage with Local Culture

Integrate elements of the local culture into the property. This could include local artwork, themed decor, or information about cultural events happening during their stay.

Seasonal Decor

Decorate the property according to seasons or holidays. Seasonal touches add a sense of festivity and make the stay more memorable.

Themed Packages

Offer themed packages for special occasions or interests. This could include a romance, adventure, or wellness package with relevant amenities and services.

Celebrate Milestones

Acknowledge guest milestones, such as anniversaries or birthdays, by leaving a small token or note in the property to make their celebration extra special.

Local Experiences Partnership

Partner with local businesses to offer unique experiences to your guests. This could include discounts for local tours, spa services, or restaurant collaborations.

Surprise and Delight

Surprise guests with unexpected touches. This could be a stocked fridge with local snacks, a handwritten note, or a surprise event during their stay.

Kids-Friendly Amenities

If your property caters to families, provide kids-friendly amenities such as games, toys, or a designated play area.

Sustainable Practices

Incorporate sustainable practices into your property. This could include eco-friendly amenities, recycling options, or information on local sustainability initiatives.

Memory Wall or Guest Book

Create a memory wall or provide a guest book where guests can share their experiences and leave notes for future visitors.

Host Social Events

Host occasional social events for guests, such as a welcome cocktail hour or a barbecue night. This fosters community and connection.

Photography Opportunities

Design spaces with unique and Instagram-worthy elements. This encourages guests to share their experiences on social media, further promoting your property.

Stay Connected After Departure

Stay connected with guests after their departure. Send a thank-you message, ask for feedback, and provide information on future promotions or events.

Focusing on these tips and consistently delivering memorable experiences can create a positive reputation for your short-term rental and encourage guests to return while recommending your property to others.

20. Handling guest reviews and feedback

Handling guest reviews and feedback is a crucial aspect of managing a short-term rental. Positive reviews can boost your property's reputation, while negative feedback presents an opportunity for improvement. Here's a guide on effectively handling guest reviews and feedback:

Monitor Reviews Regularly

Regularly monitor reviews on online platforms, booking websites, and social media.

Stay informed about what guests are saying about their experiences.

Respond Promptly

Respond promptly to all positive and negative reviews.

Aim to respond within 24 to 48 hours to show that you value guest feedback.

Express Gratitude for Positive Reviews

Express gratitude for positive reviews and highlight specific aspects the guest mentions.

Thank them for choosing your property and contributing to its positive reputation.

Address Negative Reviews Professionally

Approach negative reviews professionally and constructively.

Acknowledge the guest's concerns, apologize if necessary, and assure them that you take their feedback seriously.

Avoid Defensive Responses

Avoid defensive or aggressive responses to negative reviews.

Stay calm, address the issues objectively, and focus on finding solutions.

Apologize Sincerely

If there was an issue during the guest's stay, offer a sincere apology.

Let the guest know that their experience does not reflect your usual standards and that you are committed to addressing the issue.

Offer Solutions

Provide solutions or actions you plan to take to rectify any issues raised.

Demonstrate your commitment to improving the guest experience.

Take the Conversation Offline

If the review involves specific details or private information, suggest continuing the conversation offline.

Provide contact information for further communication.

Encourage Private FeedbackEncourage guests to provide private feedback during their stay.

This allows you to address issues before they become public reviews.

Learn from Feedback

Use guest feedback as a learning opportunity.

Identify recurring themes or patterns in reviews and make improvements to enhance the overall guest experience.

Showcase Positive Changes

If you've implemented changes based on guest feedback, showcase these improvements in your responses.

Let future guests know that you are proactive in addressing concerns.

Respond to Neutral Reviews

Even for neutral reviews, express appreciation for the guest's feedback and mention any changes or improvements you've made.

Encourage More Reviews

Encourage more guests to leave reviews by expressing the importance of their feedback.

Positive reviews can offset occasional negative ones and contribute to a more balanced overall rating.

Use Constructive Criticism

See negative feedback as an opportunity for constructive criticism.

Use it to refine and enhance your short-term rental business.

Monitor Trends and Patterns

Monitor trends and patterns in guest feedback.

Identify areas where you consistently receive positive feedback and areas that may need improvement.

Implement Continuous Improvement

Embrace a culture of continuous improvement.

Regularly assess and update your property, services, and guest interactions based on feedback.

Share Positive Feedback

Share positive guest feedback on your website, social media, or marketing materials.
Use positive testimonials to build trust and attract new guests.

Encourage Repeat Bookings

Engage with guests who left positive reviews and encourage them to return.

Offer special promotions or discounts to show appreciation for their loyalty.

Stay Professional and Courteous

Maintain a professional and courteous tone in all responses, irrespective of the nature of the review.

Show that you are receptive to feedback and committed to guest satisfaction.

Use Feedback to Enhance Marketing

Incorporate positive aspects highlighted in reviews into your marketing strategy.

Showcase unique features or experiences that guests have praised.

By actively engaging with guest reviews and feedback, you can demonstrate your commitment to guest satisfaction, make improvements where necessary, and build a positive reputation for your short-term rental. Continuous feedback management contributes to a better guest experience and increased confidence from potential guests.

6

Chapter 6: Managing Operations and Finances

21. Streamlining check-in and check-out processes

Streamlining the check-in and check-out processes for your short-term rental is essential for providing guests with a seamless and positive experience. Here are tips to help you streamline these processes

Digital Pre-Arrival Information

Send digital pre-arrival information to guests, including check-in instructions, access codes, and any other relevant details.

Provide this information well in advance to ensure guests are prepared.

Keyless Entry Systems

Consider implementing keyless entry systems or smart locks.

Keyless entry eliminates the need for physical keys and allows guests to access the property using a unique code or smartphone app.

Automated Check-In

Automate the check-in process as much as possible.

Utilize property management systems (PMS) or booking platforms that offer automated check-in features.

Clear Directions and Signage

Provide clear directions to the property, especially if it's in a complex or has multiple units.

Use signage to guide guests to the check-in location and provide instructions.

Mobile Check-In Options

Offer mobile check-in options through your booking platform or a dedicated app.

Allow guests to complete check-in procedures using their smartphones.

Self-Check-In Kiosks

If applicable, consider implementing self-check-in kiosks for guests to complete the check-in process independently.

Online Registration Forms

Use online registration forms to collect necessary guest information before arrival.
This speeds up the check-in process and minimizes paperwork.

Provide Contactless Payment Options

Offer contactless payment options to streamline the payment process during check-in.

Utilize secure online payment platforms to enhance efficiency.

Centralized Check-In Desk or Location

If managing multiple properties, consider having a centralized check-in desk or location.

This can be more convenient for guests and helps centralize your operational processes.

Automated Welcome Messages

Set up automated welcome messages to greet guests upon arrival.

Include essential information, such as WiFi codes and emergency contact details.

Concierge Service Apps

Integrate concierge service apps that provide information on local attractions, dining options, and activities.

Guests can access this information conveniently during their stay.

Express Check-Out Options

Offer express check-out options for guests who prefer a quick departure.

Provide instructions on how guests can check out without visiting a front desk.

Key Drop or Mailbox for Check-Out

Implement a key drop or mailbox system for guests to leave keys during check-out.

This allows for flexible departure times without requiring face-to-face interaction.

Automated Check-Out Surveys

Implement automated check-out surveys to collect guest feedback.

Use the feedback to improve and enhance future guest experiences.

Clear Check-Out Procedures

Clearly communicate check-out procedures, including any tasks guests must complete before leaving.

Provide information on where to leave keys or access cards.

Utilize QR Codes

Place QR codes in the property with links to important information, such as check-in instructions or property details.

Guests can scan the codes for quick access to relevant information.

Integration with Messaging Platforms

Integrate with messaging platforms to facilitate real-time communication with guests.

Address any issues or inquiries promptly to enhance the guest experience.

Digital Guest Surveys

Implement digital guest surveys after check-out to gather insights on their stay. -

Use survey results to identify areas for improvement.

Collaborate with Property Management Systems

Collaborate with property management systems offering comprehensive booking, check-in, and check-out solutions.

These systems can streamline operations and enhance overall efficiency.

By implementing these strategies, you can create a hassle-free and efficient check-in and check-out experience for your short-term rental guests. Streamlining these processes improves guest satisfaction, positive reviews, and operational efficiency.

22. Hiring cleaning and maintenance services

Hiring reliable cleaning and maintenance services is crucial for the success of your short-term rental. Here's a guide on managing this aspect efficiently

Establish Clear Cleaning Standards

Develop detailed cleaning standards for your short-term rental. Clearly outline tasks, expectations, and quality standards to ensure consistency.

Vet Cleaning Services

Research and vet cleaning services before hiring. Look for reputable companies or individual cleaners with positive reviews and experience in short-term rental cleaning.

Regular Cleaning Schedule

Implement a regular cleaning schedule that accommodates check-in and check-out times. Ensure that the property is thoroughly cleaned and prepared for each new guest.

Coordinate with Turnover Times

Coordinate with cleaning services to align with turnover times between guests. Aim for a quick turnaround to maintain a high level of guest satisfaction.

Inspect After Cleaning

Conduct inspections after each cleaning session to ensure the property meets your standards. Address any issues promptly to maintain cleanliness and presentation.

Provide a Checklist

Provide cleaning services with a detailed checklist outlining the cleaning tasks required for each property area. This helps maintain consistency.

Emergency Cleaning Services

Have a plan for emergency cleaning services. If there's a last-minute booking or an unexpected issue, ensure that you can arrange for quick and efficient cleaning.

Address Guest Feedback

Monitor guest feedback on cleanliness and address any concerns imme-diately. Use feedback to improve your cleaning processes.

Maintenance Protocols

Establish maintenance protocols for regular inspections and upkeep. This includes checking appliances, plumbing, HVAC systems, and other essential components.

Schedule Routine Maintenance

Schedule routine maintenance tasks such as HVAC servicing, pest control, and property inspections to prevent issues before they arise.

Emergency Maintenance Contacts

Keep a list of reliable and responsive maintenance professionals for emergencies. This includes plumbers, electricians, and general contrac-tors.

Communicate with Cleaning Staff

Maintain open communication with your cleaning staff. Provide clear instructions, share feedback, and address any issues promptly to foster a positive working relationship.

Consider Green Cleaning Practices

If possible, consider implementing green cleaning practices. This aligns with sustainability trends and may appeal to environmentally conscious guests.

Professional Training

Provide professional training for cleaning staff to ensure they understand the specific requirements and standards for short-term rental properties.

Evaluate Pricing Structure

Evaluate the pricing structure of your cleaning and maintenance services. Ensure that it aligns with your budget while providing quality services.

Set Clear Expectations

Set clear expectations with cleaning and maintenance services regarding your standards, scheduling, and any specific requirements unique to your property.

Insurance and Bonding

Ensure that your cleaning and maintenance services are insured and bonded. This protects them in case of accidents or damages during their work.

Regularly Review Contracts

Review contracts with cleaning and maintenance services to ensure that terms, pricing, and expectations are up-to-date and in line with your needs.

Maintain a Spare Key System

Implement a secure spare key system with your cleaning and maintenance staff. This ensures efficient access when needed.

Continuous Improvement

Continuously assess the performance of your cleaning and maintenance services. Seek feedback from guests and staff to identify areas for improvement.

Implementing these strategies ensures that your short-term rental is consistently clean, well-maintained, and ready to welcome guests. Reliable cleaning and maintenance services contribute significantly to positive guest experiences and help maintain a strong reputation for your property.

23. Budgeting and financial management

Effectively managing the budget and finances for your short-term rental is crucial for long-term success. Here's a guide on budgeting and financial management for short-term rentals

Establish a Comprehensive Budget

Create a detailed budget that includes all potential expenses related to your short-term rental. This should cover operational costs, maintenance, utilities, marketing, and other relevant categories.

Identify Fixed and Variable Costs

Differentiate between fixed costs (e.g., mortgage, property taxes) and variable costs (e.g., cleaning fees, utility bills). Understanding these distinctions helps in better financial planning.

Pricing Strategy

Develop a pricing strategy based on market research, seasonality, and demand patterns. Set competitive rates that cover your expenses and generate a profit.

Emergency Fund

Establish an emergency fund for unexpected expenses or periods of low occupancy. Having a financial cushion can help you manage unforeseen challenges.

Track Income and Expenses

Implement a robust system to track income and expenses accurately. Utilize accounting software or tools to maintain organized financial records.

Reserve for Maintenance and Repairs

Allocate funds for regular maintenance and potential repairs. Proactive maintenance can prevent costly issues in the long run.

Tax Planning

Work with a tax professional to understand tax implications related to short-term rentals. Explore deductions and credits available to property owners in your region.

Insurance Coverage

Ensure you have appropriate insurance coverage for your short-term rental property. This includes property insurance, liability coverage, and coverage for short-term rental activities.

Marketing Budget

Allocate a portion of your budget for marketing efforts. This may include online advertising, professional photography, and promotional materials to attract guests.

Utility Efficiency

Implement energy-efficient practices to reduce utility costs. Consider using smart thermostats, energy-efficient appliances, and LED lighting.

Monitor Occupancy

Keep a close eye on occupancy rates. Analyze trends to identify peak seasons and optimize pricing during high-demand periods.

Contingency Planning

Develop contingency plans for various scenarios, such as economic downturns, changes in local regulations, or unexpected market fluctuations.

Negotiate Vendor Contracts

Negotiate contracts with vendors, such as cleaning services and maintenance professionals, to secure competitive rates and favorable terms.

Review and Adjust

Regularly review your budget and financial performance. Adjust your budget as needed based on changing market conditions and business dynamics.

Financial Goals

Set financial goals for your short-term rental business. This could include revenue targets, occupancy rates, or return on investment (ROI) goals.

Seasonal Variations

Account for seasonal variations in your budget. Plan for increased expenses during peak seasons and adjust accordingly during slower periods.

Upgrade Investments Wisely

Prioritize upgrades or investments that have a tangible impact on guest satisfaction and property value. Evaluate the return on investment for each improvement.

Monitor Competition

Keep an eye on your competitors in the short-term rental market. Stay informed about their pricing strategies, amenities, and guest reviews to stay competitive.

Financial Reporting

Generate regular financial reports to assess the performance of your short-term rental. This includes income statements, balance sheets, and cash flow statements.

Professional Advice

Seek advice from financial professionals, such as accountants or financial advisors, to ensure that your budgeting and financial management strategies align with best practices.

By implementing these budgeting and financial management practices, you can maintain a healthy financial position for your short-term rental business. Regularly assess your financial performance, adapt to market changes, and make informed decisions to optimize your property's financial success.

24. Tax considerations for short-term rental income

Tax considerations for short-term rental income are essential for property owners to understand and comply with tax obligations. Here's a guide to help you navigate the tax landscape for short-term rentals:

Rental Income Reporting

Report all rental income on your tax return, including income from short-term rentals. This includes income from online platforms, cash, or other methods.

Deductible Expenses

Identify and track deductible expenses associated with your short-term rental. Common deductions include property management fees, cleaning fees, utilities, property taxes, mortgage interest, and maintenance costs.

Depreciation

Consider claiming depreciation on your rental property. Depreciation allows you to deduct the cost of the property over time, reducing your taxable income.

Home Office Deduction

If you use part of your home exclusively for your short-term rental business, you may qualify for a home office deduction. This deduction can include a portion of your mortgage, utilities, and other related expenses.

State and Local Taxes

Be aware of state and local tax obligations. Some jurisdictions may impose additional taxes or fees on short-term rentals, such as occupancy taxes or sales taxes.

Transient Occupancy Taxes (TOT)

Many areas require hosts to collect and remit transient occupancy taxes (TOT) from guests. Familiarize yourself with local TOT regulations and ensure compliance.

Record-Keeping

Maintain thorough and accurate records of all income and expenses related to your short-term rental. This documentation is crucial for tax reporting and potential audits.

Form 1099 Reporting

If you use a platform like Airbnb, it may issue a Form 1099-K to report your income to the IRS. Be sure to reconcile this information with your records.

Self-Employment Taxes

Short-term rental income is generally considered self-employment income. Be prepared to pay self-employment taxes on your net rental income.

Qualified Business Income Deduction (QBI)

Depending on your eligibility, you may qualify for the QBI deduction, which allows eligible taxpayers to deduct up to 20% of qualified business income.

Tax Professional Consultation

Consult with a tax professional or accountant familiar with short-term rental tax regulations. They can provide personalized advice based on your specific situation.

Estimated Quarterly Payments

If your tax liability is expected to be significant, consider making estimated quarterly tax payments to avoid underpayment penalties.

Non-Refundable Credits

Explore tax credits that may apply to your short-term rental business, such as energy-efficient property credits or credits for making improvements for accessibility.

Personal Use of Property

Understand the tax implications of using the property for personal purposes. The ability to deduct certain expenses may be affected by the percentage of time the property is used for personal use versus rental use.

Keep Abreast of Tax Law Changes

Stay informed about tax laws that may impact short-term rental income. Tax regulations can evolve, so staying up-to-date is crucial.

Forming a Business Entity

Depending on your circumstances, forming a business entity like an LLC may provide certain tax benefits and liability protection. Consult with a legal and tax professional to assess the best structure for your situation.

Record Short-Term Rental Days

Track the number of days your property is rented as a short-term rental. Some tax benefits, like the ability to claim certain deductions, may depend on the percentage of days the property is rented.

Rental Loss Limitations

Be aware of limitations on claiming rental losses. The IRS has rules regarding the ability to deduct losses from rental activities, and these rules may vary based on factors like active participation.

Document Rental Property Improvements

Keep detailed records of any improvements made to the rental property. Some improvements may be eligible for depreciation or other tax benefits.

Seek Professional Guidance for Specifics

Tax laws can be complex and subject to change. Seek professional guidance to ensure compliance with current regulations and maximize available deductions.

Remember that tax considerations for short-term rental income may vary based on your location, the nature of your rental business, and changes in tax laws. Consultation with tax professionals is highly recommended to effectively navigate your specific tax obligations.

7

Chapter 7: Legal and Regulatory Compliance

25. Navigating local regulations and zoning laws

Navigating local regulations and zoning laws for short-term rentals is crucial to ensure compliance with local ordinances and avoid legal issues. Here's a guide on navigating these regulations

Research Local Zoning Laws

Start by researching local zoning laws and regulations that pertain to short-term rentals. Zoning laws dictate how properties can be used in specific areas, and violations can result in fines or legal action.

Contact Local Planning or Zoning Departments

Reach out to your local planning or zoning department to obtain information on regulations specific to short-term rentals. They can guide applicable zoning codes and any restrictions.

Attend Local Meetings or Workshops

Attend local community meetings or workshops to stay informed about potential zoning laws and regulations changes. Being involved in local discussions can help you anticipate and adapt to any new developments.

Identify Permitted Zones

Determine which zones in your area permit short-term rentals. Some zones may have restrictions or require special permits, while others may prohibit short-term rentals altogether.

Obtain Necessary Permits and Licenses

If permits or licenses are required for short-term rentals, ensure that you obtain them. This may involve submitting applications, paying fees, and meeting specific criteria set by the local authorities.

Understand Occupancy Limits

Be aware of any occupancy limits imposed by local regulations. Some areas may restrict the number of guests allowed in short-term rental properties.

Compliance with Building Codes

Ensure that your short-term rental property complies with local building codes and safety regulations. This includes fire safety, accessibility, and other structural requirements.

Check for Noise Restrictions

Check if local ordinances impose noise restrictions or quiet hours. Inform guests of any noise regulations to avoid disturbances to neighbors.

Set Clear House Rules

Establish clear house rules for your short-term rental property. Communicate these rules to guests and include them in rental agreements to reinforce compliance with local regulations.

Monitor Changes in Regulations

Stay vigilant for any changes in local regulations. Zoning laws and short-term rental ordinances may evolve, so regularly check for updates that may impact your business.

Join Local Host Associations

Join local host associations or networks. These groups often provide valuable information, support, and advocacy for short-term rental hosts facing regulatory challenges.

Consult with Legal Professionals

If you're uncertain about local regulations or face legal challenges, consult with legal professionals specializing in real estate and local zoning laws. They can provide specific guidance tailored to your situation.

Be Transparent with Neighbors

Foster positive relationships with neighbors by being transparent about your short-term rental business. Address their concerns and emphasize your commitment to being a responsible host.

Comply with Tax Requirements

Ensure compliance with local tax requirements for short-term rentals. This may include collecting and remitting occupancy taxes or other local taxes.

Monitor Online Platforms Policies

Be aware of and comply with policies set by online platforms (e.g., Airbnb, Vrbo) that you use for listing your short-term rental. Platforms may have their own rules and requirements.

Explore Conditional Use Permits

In some cases, you may need to apply for a conditional use permit to operate a short-term rental in a zone that is not explicitly permitted. Consult with local authorities on the application process.

Neighborhood Covenants and Restrictions

Check for any neighborhood covenants, conditions, and restrictions (CC&Rs) that may affect your short-term rental. These are rules established by homeowners' associations or community groups.

Utilize Advocacy Groups

Explore or join local advocacy groups that support responsible short-term rental hosting. These groups can provide resources and guidance on navigating regulatory challenges.

Establish a Communication Plan

Establish a communication plan with neighbors to address any issues. An open communication line can prevent conflicts and promote a positive neighborhood environment.

Professional Property Management

Consider hiring a professional property management company that is familiar with local regulations. Property managers can help ensure compliance and handle day-to-day operational matters.

Navigating local regulations and zoning laws requires thorough research, proactive communication, and a commitment to compliance. By staying informed and taking the necessary steps to adhere to local requirements, you can successfully operate your short-term rental business while maintaining positive relationships with the local community.

26. Understanding short-term rental platforms' policies

Understanding the policies of short-term rental platforms is crucial for hosts to operate within the platform's guidelines and provide a positive experience for guests. Here's a guide on key aspects to consider when understanding short-term rental platforms' policies

Terms of Service and User Agreement

Start by thoroughly reading and understanding the platform's Terms of Service or User Agreement. This document outlines the rules and regulations that hosts and guests must adhere to while using the platform.

Listing Guidelines

Review the platform's guidelines for creating and managing listings. This includes rules about accurate property descriptions, pricing transparency, and photo quality.

Booking and Reservation Policies

Understand the platform's policies regarding booking procedures, reservation confirmations, and cancellation policies. This helps you manage reservations by following the platform's rules.

Host Standards and Expectations

Familiarize yourself with the platform's expectations for hosts. This may include guidelines on cleanliness, communication with guests, and providing a positive experience.

Communication Policies

Be aware of the platform's communication policies. Understand how and when you can communicate with guests and use the platform's messaging system for official communication.

Payment and Transaction Policies

Understand the platform's payment and transaction policies. This includes details about payment processing, payout schedules, and any fees associated with hosting.

Verification and Identity Checks

Learn about the platform's verification and identity check processes. Many platforms require hosts to verify their identity and may offer enhanced features for verified hosts.

Local Regulations and Compliance

Platforms may have specific policies regarding compliance with local regulations, zoning laws, and taxes. Ensure that your listing adheres to these rules to avoid any violations.

Guest Reviews and Ratings

Understand how the platform's review and rating system works. En-courage guests to leave reviews and respond professionally to feedback, as reviews can impact your listing's visibility.

Safety and Security Guidelines

Familiarize yourself with the safety and security guidelines provided by the platform. This includes recommendations on key exchange, property access, and emergency procedures.

Nondiscrimination Policies

Be aware of the platform's nondiscrimination policies. Short-term rental platforms typically have strict policies against discrimination based on factors such as race, gender, or sexual orientation.

Use of Professional Photography

Some platforms encourage hosts to use professional-quality photos for their listings. Understand the platform's recommendations regarding listing visuals and invest in high-quality images.

Changes to Policies

Keep an eye on updates and changes to the platform's policies. Plat-forms may occasionally revise their terms and conditions, and staying informed about any modifications is important.

Use of Instant Booking

If the platform offers an instant booking feature, understand how it works and whether you want to enable it for your listing. Instant booking allows guests to book without host approval.

Hosting Eligibility Requirements

Ensure you meet the platform's hosting eligibility requirements. This may include age restrictions, background checks, or other criteria set by the platform.

Handling Guest Issues and Disputes

Understand the platform's procedures for handling guest issues, disputes, or conflicts. Familiarize yourself with the resolution process outlined by the platform.

Responsible Hosting Practices

Platforms often emphasize responsible hosting practices. This may include guidelines on respecting neighbors, promoting a safe environment, and complying with local laws.

Prohibited Activities

Review the platform's list of prohibited activities. This can include hosting unauthorized events, engaging in illegal activities, or violating the platform's policies.

Reporting Violations

Know the process for reporting violations by guests or other hosts. If you encounter any issues that violate platform policies, report them to the platform's support team.

Support and Assistance

Understand how to contact the platform's support team. Familiarize yourself with the available resources, help centers, and customer support channels.

By thoroughly understanding and following the policies set by short-term rental platforms, hosts can create a positive and compliant hosting experience for themselves and their guests. Staying informed and following platform guidelines contributes to a successful and responsible hosting experience.

27. Insurance considerations for short-term rentals

Insurance is a critical aspect of managing short-term rentals, providing property owners and guests protection. Here are key insurance considerations for short-term rentals

Homeowners Insurance Review

Contact your homeowners insurance provider and inform them that you plan to use your property for short-term rentals. Standard homeowners insurance may not cover commercial activities like short-term rentals.

Specialized Short-Term Rental Insurance

Consider obtaining specialized short-term rental insurance. This type of insurance is designed to cover the risks associated with renting out your property short-term.

Liability Insurance

Ensure your insurance policy includes liability coverage. Liability insurance protects you in case a guest is injured on your property or if their property is damaged, and they hold you responsible.

Property Damage Coverage

Confirm that the insurance policy covers property damage. This can include damage caused by guests or other covered events.

Loss of Income Coverage

Look for policies that offer loss of income coverage. This coverage can compensate you for lost rental income if your property becomes uninhabitable due to a covered event, such as a fire or natural disaster.

Insurance for Belongings

If you provide furnishings or personal property in your rental, make sure your insurance policy includes contents coverage. This can protect your belongings from damage or theft.

Business Interruption Coverage

Consider adding business interruption coverage to your insurance policy. This coverage can provide financial protection if your short-term rental business is interrupted due to a covered event.

Check Airbnb or Vrbo Host Guarantee/Protection

If you list your property on platforms like Airbnb or Vrbo, be aware of their host guarantee or host protection programs. While these programs can provide additional coverage, they are not a substitute for a comprehensive insurance policy.

Communicate Changes to Insurance Provider

Keep your insurance provider informed of any changes, such as renovations or upgrades to your property. This ensures that your coverage is accurate and up to date.

Review Exclusions and Limitations

Carefully review the exclusions and limitations of your insurance policy. Some policies may have specific exclusions for certain events or types of damage.

Understand Airbnb Host Liability Insurance

If you host on Airbnb, be aware of the Host Liability Insurance program, which provides primary liability coverage for up to $1 million per occurrence. However, this is not a substitute for comprehensive insurance.

Security Measures

Implement security measures in your property, such as smoke detectors, fire extinguishers, and security systems. Some insurance providers may offer discounts for properties with enhanced safety features.

Check Local Regulations

Be aware of local regulations that may require specific insurance coverage for short-term rentals. Some areas may have insurance requirements for hosts.

Personal Injury Coverage

Ensure that your insurance policy includes personal injury coverage. This can protect you if a guest claims injury due to a property-related issue.

Guest Property Coverage

Consider policies that offer coverage for guest property. This can protect guests' belongings in case of damage or theft during their stay.

Understand Deductibles

Review the deductibles associated with your insurance policy. Understand the amount you would be responsible for in the event of a claim.

Umbrella Insurance

Consider obtaining umbrella insurance for additional liability coverage. This type of insurance can provide extra protection beyond the limits of your primary policies.

Consult with an Insurance Professional

Consult with an insurance professional specializing in short-term rental insurance. They can help you understand your specific needs and find a policy that provides adequate coverage.

Document Property Condition

Document the condition of your property before and after a guest stays. This documentation can be valuable in the event of a claim.

Regular Policy Reviews

Regularly review and update your insurance policy to ensure that it continues to meet your needs. Changes in your property or hosting practices may require adjustments to your coverage.

By addressing these insurance considerations, you can help protect your property, your guests, and your financial interests while operating a short-term rental business. It's crucial to communicate openly with your insurance provider and stay informed about the coverage options available to you.

28. Handling disputes and conflicts with guests

Handling disputes and conflicts with short-term rental guests is an inevitable aspect of hosting. Effectively managing these situations is crucial for maintaining a positive guest experience and protecting your reputation. Here's a guide on handling disputes and conflicts

Preventative Measures

Implement clear house rules Establish comprehensive house rules that cover important aspects such as noise levels, check-in/check-out times, and property use.

Set expectations in your listing Communicate expectations in your property listing regarding house rules, policies, and any specific details guests should be aware of.

Open Communication

Respond promptly Address guest inquiries and concerns to demonstrate your commitment to their satisfaction.

Be transparent Communicate openly with guests about any issues or changes, providing clear and honest information.

Professionalism

Maintain professionalism Approach conflicts calmly and professionally. Avoid emotional reactions and focus on finding solutions.

Documentation

Keep records Document all communication with guests. This includes messages, emails, and any agreements made before or during their stay.

Understand the Issue

Gather information Obtain a clear understanding of the guest's perspective and the nature of the dispute. Listen actively and ask questions to gather relevant details.

Offer Solutions

Propose solutions Present potential solutions to the guest based on the nature of the issue. This can include refunds, discounts, or alternative arrangements.

Consult Platform Policies

Review platform policies Familiarize yourself with the dispute resolution process outlined by the hosting platform. Follow the platform's guidelines for addressing conflicts.

Involve Mediation Services

Consider mediation services Some platforms offer mediation services to help hosts and guests resolve disputes. Utilize these services if needed.

Maintain Guest Privacy

Respect privacy Ensure that any communication regarding the dispute maintains the guest's privacy. Avoid discussing sensitive issues publicly.

Seek Legal Advice if Necessary

Consult legal advice If a dispute escalates, seek legal advice to understand your rights and responsibilities. Consider involving legal professionals if necessary.

Learn from Feedback

Learn from feedback. Use disputes as opportunities for improvement. If there are recurring issues, consider making changes to prevent similar conflicts in the future.

Respond Professionally to Reviews

Address reviews professionally. If the guest leaves a negative review, respond professionally and express a willingness to address the issue. Future guests will see your responsiveness.

Have a Contingency Plan

Develop a contingency plan. Be prepared for common issues by having a contingency plan. This can include alternative accommodations or quick solutions to common problems.

Insurance Coverage

Consult your insurance If the dispute involves property damage, consult your insurance provider to understand coverage and initiate a claim if necessary.

Stay Informed About Local Laws

Know local laws Familiarize yourself with local laws that may impact dispute resolution, especially if legal action becomes necessary.

Take Preventive Action

Learn from previous disputes Analyze past disputes to identify patterns and take preventive action. This could involve adjusting policies, improving communication, or enhancing guest education.

Engage with Online Communities

Seek advice from peers. Engage with online communities or forums where hosts share experiences and advice. Learning from others who have faced similar challenges can be valuable.

Clarify Expectations

Set clear expectations Communicate expectations to guests before their arrival. Ensure they understand your house rules and policies.

Implement a Guest Agreement

Use a guest agreement Consider implementing a guest agreement that outlines expectations and responsibilities. Having a written agreement can help prevent misunderstandings.

Continuous Improvement

Learn and adapt Use each dispute as an opportunity for continuous improvement. Evaluate the situation, gather feedback, and adjust to enhance the guest experience.

Handling disputes and conflicts is part of the hosting experience, and addressing them professionally can lead to favorable resolutions. You can navigate conflicts effectively and maintain a positive hosting reputation by proactively managing communication, understanding the guest's perspective, and seeking constructive solutions.

8

Chapter 8: Scaling Your Short-Term Rental Business

29. Expanding your portfolio

*Expanding your short-term rental portfolio requires careful planning, re-
search, and strategic decision-making. Here's a guide to help you grow your
short-term rental business*

Market Research

Conduct thorough market research to identify potential locations for
expansion. Analyze demand, competition, and local regulations to make
informed decisions.

Financial Analysis

Assess your financial capacity and determine the budget for acquiring new properties. Consider factors such as property prices, renovation costs, and potential returns on investment.

Diversification

Consider diversifying your portfolio by targeting different types of properties or locations. This can help minimize risk and appeal to a broader range of guests.

Optimize Existing Properties

Ensure your existing properties are optimized for maximum profitability. Enhance amenities, update furnishings, and improve the overall guest experience to increase rental income.

Networking

Build a real estate and short-term rental industry network. Connect with local real estate agents, property managers, and other hosts to stay informed about potential opportunities.

Local Regulations

Understand local regulations and zoning laws in the areas where you plan to expand. Compliance with regulations is crucial for a successful short-term rental business.

Professional Advice

Seek advice from real estate professionals, financial advisors, and legal experts. Their insights can help you navigate the complexities of property acquisition and management.

Evaluate Return on Investment (ROI)

Calculate the potential return on investment for each property you consider. Assess factors such as rental income, property appreciation, and ongoing expenses.

Financing Options

Explore financing options for property acquisition. This may include traditional mortgages, investment loans, or other financing methods. Evaluate interest rates and terms to choose the most suitable option.

Strategic Partnerships

Explore partnerships with property management companies or real estate professionals. Partnering with experts in the field can streamline property acquisition and management processes.

Scalable Systems

Implement scalable systems for managing multiple properties. Invest in property management software and processes that can efficiently handle a growing portfolio.

Employee or Outsourcing

Assess whether you need additional help to manage an expanded portfolio. Consider hiring employees or outsourcing tasks such as cleaning, maintenance, and guest communication.

Technology Integration

Embrace technology to streamline operations. Use smart home devices for keyless entry, automated check-ins, and other features that enhance guest experience and property management.

Monitoring Trends

Stay informed about industry trends and changing guest preferences. Adapting to market trends can give you a competitive edge in attracting guests.

Marketing Strategy

Develop a robust marketing strategy for your expanded portfolio. Use online platforms, social media, and professional photography to showcase your properties effectively.

Customer Feedback

Pay attention to guest feedback and reviews. Use this information to continually improve your properties and services, ensuring high guest satisfaction.

Adapt to Seasonal Demand

Consider the seasonality of your target locations. Adjust pricing and marketing strategies based on seasonal demand to optimize occupancy rates.

Legal Considerations

Ensure compliance with all legal and tax considerations associated with property acquisition and short-term rentals in different locations.

Risk Management

Implement risk management strategies to mitigate potential property ownership and short-term rental management challenges.

Long-Term Vision

Develop a long-term vision for your short-term rental business. Consider how each property fits into your overall strategy and contributes to the growth and success of your portfolio.

Expanding your short-term rental portfolio requires a combination of financial acumen, market knowledge, and effective management practices. By carefully planning and executing each step, you can grow your business successfully and capitalize on opportunities in the dynamic short-term rental market.

30. Hiring a property management team

Hiring a property management team for short-term rentals can be a strategic decision to streamline operations, enhance guest experiences, and ensure the smooth running of your rental business. Here's a guide on how to hire and work with a property management team for short-term rentals

Define Your Needs

Clearly outline your expectations and needs for the property management team. Determine whether you need assistance with guest communication, cleaning services, maintenance, marketing, or a combination.

Research and Interview

Research local property management companies or individuals with experience in short-term rentals. Conduct interviews to assess their expertise, services, and compatibility with your business goals.

Check References

Ask for references from other property owners who have worked with the property management team. This can provide insights into their reputation, reliability, and overall performance.

Legal Considerations

Ensure that the property management team is knowledgeable about local regulations and compliance requirements for short-term rentals. Compliance with laws and zoning regulations is crucial.

Service Agreement

Clearly define the terms of the service agreement. Include details such as services provided, fees, responsibilities, and any performance metrics you want the team to meet.

Communication Protocols

Establish communication protocols with the property management team. Clearly define how communication will be handled, what information needs to be shared, and the frequency of updates.

Technology Integration

Ensure the property management team uses technology to streamline operations. This can include property management software, booking platforms, and smart home devices for keyless entry and automation.

Pricing Structure

Understand the pricing structure of the property management team. Some may charge a percentage of rental income, a flat fee, or a combination of both. Evaluate the cost-effectiveness of their services.

Performance Metrics

Establish performance metrics to evaluate the effectiveness of the property management team. This could include occupancy rates, guest satisfaction scores, and response times to guest inquiries.

Maintenance and Cleaning Standards

Communicate your property maintenance and cleanliness standards. Ensure that the property management team follows these standards to maintain the quality of your short-term rentals.

Emergency Response Plan

Develop an emergency response plan with the property management team. Clearly outline procedures for handling urgent situations, such as property damage, emergencies, or guest issues.

Guest Communication

Define the process for guest communication. Specify how the property management team will handle check-ins, check-outs, and any guest inquiries or issues that may arise during a stay.

Marketing Strategies

Collaborate on marketing strategies to attract guests. Discuss how the property management team can optimize listings, implement pricing strategies, and use online platforms to maximize property visibility.

Regular Reporting

Request regular reports from the property management team. This can include financial reports, occupancy rates, and summaries of guest feedback. Regular reporting keeps you informed about the performance of your short-term rentals.

Flexibility and Adaptability

Choose a property management team that is flexible and adaptable. The ability to adjust to changing market conditions, guest preferences, and unforeseen challenges is crucial for success.

Conflict Resolution

Establish protocols for conflict resolution. Clearly outline how the property management team should handle disputes with guests, neighbors, or any other issues that may arise.

Insurance Coverage

Confirm that the property management team has appropriate insurance coverage. This may include liability insurance and coverage for property damage caused by their services.

Regular Check-ins

Schedule regular check-ins with the property management team to discuss performance, address any concerns, and align strategies for improvement.

Continuous Training

Provide ongoing training to the property management team to update them on industry trends, regulation changes, and best practices for short-term rental management.

Exit Strategy

Include an exit strategy in the service agreement. Define the process for terminating the agreement if necessary, and ensure that you retain control over your properties in case you decide to part ways with the property management team.

Hiring a property management team for short-term rentals can significantly alleviate the workload and enhance the efficiency of your business. By establishing clear expectations, communication channels, and performance metrics, you can build a successful partnership that contributes to the growth and success of your short-term rental portfolio.

31. Exploring partnerships and collaborations

Exploring partnerships and collaborations for your short-term rental can offer various benefits, from expanding your reach to enhancing guest experiences. Here's a guide on exploring and establishing partnerships for your short-term rental business

Identify Potential Partners

Identify companies or individuals that align with your short-term rental business. This could include local businesses, tourism organizations, event organizers, or complementary service providers.

Local Businesses

Reach out to local businesses such as restaurants, cafes, tour operators, and attractions. Explore partnership opportunities to enhance the guest experience and add value.

Tourism Organizations

Connect with your area's tourism organizations or chambers of commerce. Collaborate on promotions, local events, or marketing campaigns that showcase your short-term rental as part of the local experience.

Event Organizers

Partner with event organizers for local festivals, conferences, or special events. Provide accommodations for attendees and explore promotional collaborations to attract guests during specific events.

Complementary Services

Explore partnerships with businesses that offer complementary services, such as transportation, grocery delivery, or cleaning services. Collaborating with these services can enhance the convenience for your guests.

Online Platforms and Booking Sites

Consider listing your short-term rental on multiple online platforms and booking sites to increase visibility. Collaborate with these platforms to take advantage of promotional opportunities or features that can boost your listing.

Professional Photography and Virtual Tours

Collaborate with professional photographers and virtual tour providers to enhance the visual appeal of your property. High-quality visuals can attract more guests and contribute to better conversion rates.

Local Guides and Recommendations

Partner with local guides or influencers who can provide recommendations and insights about the area. Their recommendations can add value to the guest experience and encourage bookings.

Collaborative Marketing Campaigns

Explore joint marketing campaigns with local businesses or tourism boards. This could include co-branded promotions, social media campaigns, or collaborative content creation.

Cross-Promotions

Engage in cross-promotions with partners. For example, offer discounts or special packages for guests who use specific services or visit partner businesses.

Discounts and Special Offers

Negotiate discounts or special offers with partners for your guests. This could include discounts on local activities, dining, or transportation services.

Affiliate Programs

Explore affiliate programs with businesses that complement your short-term rental. This can involve earning a commission for each guest referral or collaborating on joint marketing efforts.

Community Engagement

Engage with the local community through collaborations. Sponsor local events, participate in community initiatives, and establish a positive presence that resonates with both guests and locals.

Networking Events

Attend networking events in your area to connect with potential partners. Networking provides opportunities to build relationships with local businesses and explore potential collaborations.

Property Management Partnerships

Explore partnerships with property management companies specializing in short-term rentals. They can assist with property management tasks, guest communication, and overall efficiency.

Guest Loyalty Programs

Collaborate on guest loyalty programs with partners. Offer incentives for guests to return by providing discounts or exclusive perks in collaboration with local businesses.

Guest Packages

Create guest packages in collaboration with partners. For example, offer themed packages that include local businesses' experiences, services, or products.

Community Events and Workshops

Host community events or workshops in collaboration with local businesses. This can create a sense of community around your short-term rental and attract guests interested in local experiences.

Feedback and Improvement

Seek feedback from guests about partner collaborations. Use this information to improve and refine your partnerships for better guest satisfaction continuously.

Legal Agreements

Establish clear legal agreements with partners. Clearly outline the terms of collaboration, expectations, and any financial arrangements to ensure a transparent and mutually beneficial partnership.

Exploring partnerships and collaborations can enhance the overall guest experience, differentiate your short-term rental, and contribute to the success and growth of your business. By fostering positive relationships within the local community and strategically aligning with complementary businesses, you can create a unique and appealing offering for your guests.

32. Diversifying into different markets

For short-term rentals can be a strategic move to maximize opportunities, reduce risk, and appeal to a broader audience. Here's a guide on diversifying your short-term rental business into different markets

Market Research

Conduct comprehensive market research to identify potential markets for expansion. Analyze factors such as demand, competition, local attractions, and regulatory environments.

Identify Target Markets

Identify specific target markets based on your research. Consider demographics, traveler preferences, and the types of guests you want to attract.

Local Regulations

Understand and comply with local regulations in each target market. Ensure that you know zoning laws, licensing requirements, and any other legal considerations for short-term rentals.

Property Selection

Select properties that align with the preferences of each target market. Consider factors such as property size, amenities, and location to meet the specific needs of different guest segments.

Adapt Marketing Strategies

Customize your marketing strategies for each target market. Tailor your listings, promotions, and messaging to appeal to unique characteristics and preferences.

Pricing Strategies

Develop competitive pricing strategies that reflect the local market conditions. Consider seasonal variations, local events, and demand patterns when setting prices.

Local Partnerships

Establish partnerships with local businesses and service providers in each market. Collaborate on promotions, offer local recommendations, and create a network that enhances the guest experience.

Cultural Sensitivity

Be culturally sensitive in your approach to each market. Understand local customs, preferences, and sensitivities to ensure that your short-term rental is welcoming to guests from different backgrounds.

Multilingual Communication

Consider providing multilingual communication to accommodate guests from different linguistic backgrounds. Ensure that your communication channels are accessible to a diverse audience.

Seasonal Considerations

Recognize and adapt to seasonal variations in each market. Some markets may have peak seasons at different times of the year, and adjusting your strategy accordingly can optimize occupancy rates.

Localized Guest Services

Offer localized guest services that cater to the unique needs of each market. This could include providing information on local attractions, transportation options, and cultural experiences.

Technology Integration

Integrate technology to streamline operations across different markets. Use property management software and booking platforms for centralized management and efficient communication.

Adapt to Local Trends

Stay informed about local trends in each market. Adapt your short-term rental offerings to align with popular trends and preferences, ensuring your properties remain appealing to guests.

Feedback and Improvement

Solicit feedback from guests in each market and continuously use this information to improve your offerings. Implement changes based on the specific preferences and expectations of each audience.

Comprehensive Marketing Campaigns

Develop extensive marketing campaigns highlighting each property's unique features in different markets. Utilize online platforms, social media, and local advertising to reach diverse audiences.

Legal Considerations

Ensure you are aware of and compliant with local legal considerations in each market. Stay informed about any regulation changes that may impact your short-term rental operations.

Localized Amenities

Consider offering localized amenities that cater to guests' interests in each market. This could include providing equipment for outdoor activities, cultural experiences, or special services.

Strategic Partnerships

Explore partnerships with local travel agencies, event organizers, or tour operators. Collaborate on packages and promotions that encourage guests to choose your short-term rentals for their travel needs.

Community Engagement

Engage with the local community in each market. Participate in community events, support local initiatives, and establish a positive presence that resonates with guests and locals.

Monitor and Adjust

Continuously monitor the performance of your short-term rentals in different markets. Track occupancy rates, guest satisfaction, and market trends, and be ready to adjust your strategies accordingly.

Diversifying into other markets requires careful planning, adaptability, and a deep understanding of the unique characteristics of each location. By tailoring your approach to the preferences and needs of different audiences, you can create a diversified short-term rental portfolio that appeals to a wide range of guests.

33. Using AI

Using AI to manage short-term rentals can streamline operations, improve guest experiences, and optimize overall efficiency. Here's a step-by-step guide on how to leverage AI for short-term rental management:

Dynamic Pricing Tools

Implement AI-powered dynamic pricing tools that analyze market demand, competitor pricing, and historical data.

Allow the tool to adjust your rental rates in real time based on factors like local events, seasonality, and demand fluctuations.

Automated Guest Communication

Utilize AI-driven chatbots for automated communication with guests.

Implement chatbots to handle common queries, provide information about the property, and assist with check-in/check-out processes.

Predictive Maintenance

Deploy AI algorithms to predict maintenance needs in your property.

Analyze historical data to anticipate when appliances or systems might require attention, enabling proactive maintenance.

Guest Personalization

Use AI to analyze guest data, preferences, and behaviors.

Provide personalized recommendations and experiences based on individual guest profiles to enhance satisfaction.

Security and Fraud Detection

Integrate AI-based security systems to detect unusual patterns or behaviors that may indicate fraudulent activity.

Enhance overall property security using AI-driven surveillance and monitoring tools.

Property Management Systems (PMS)

Adopt a property management system with AI capabilities.
    Choose a PMS that automates tasks such as booking management, cleaning schedules, and inventory tracking.

Market Trend Analysis

Leverage AI to analyze market trends, local events, and competitor strategies.

Use insights to adjust marketing strategies, pricing, and promotional activities.

Occupancy Forecasting

Implement predictive analytics to forecast occupancy rates.

Use these forecasts to plan marketing efforts, optimize pricing, and manage resources effectively.

Energy Efficiency Solutions

Integrate smart home technologies and AI to optimize energy consumption.

Use AI to control heating, cooling, and lighting systems based on occupancy, reducing energy costs.

Sentiment Analysis for Reviews

Apply AI for sentiment analysis of guest reviews.

Gain insights into guest satisfaction levels, identify areas for improvement, and respond proactively to feedback.

Data Security and Privacy

Ensure compliance with data security and privacy regulations when using AI tools.

Safeguard guest information and maintain transparency about data usage.

Remember to select AI tools that align with your specific needs and integrate seamlessly into your existing management processes. Regularly update and optimize your AI systems to stay current with technological advancements and industry trends.

Conclusion

Congratulations on completing this guide to profitable short-term rentals. By implementing the strategies and insights in this book, you are well on your way to maximizing your income and creating a successful short-term rental business. Remember, the key to sustained profitability lies in continuous learning, adaptability, and a commitment to delivering exceptional guest experiences. Happy hosting!
Mikki Wyatt

Please share your thoughts on my book on Amazon. Your feedback will make a difference and help other Short-term Rental owners find this resource.

Share your thoughts and feelings, and highlight what you feel will help you the most. Help others by giving a star rating and expressing why others should pick up this book. Let's build the Short-term rental market even better, one book at a time!

Watch for other resources coming soon! Send me an email to be on my resource list: mikkicwyatt@gmail.com